Blackburn
College

Library
01254 292120

Please return this book on or before the last date below

Le

Socia
All p
econd
they
specif

The E
consc
in see
of the
BASW
in soc
ture.
and tl
books.
framev
discuss
and h
practit

wide variety of experience.

JO CAMPLING

s in this series follows overleaf

PRACTICAL SOCIAL WORK

Social Work and Empowerment
Robert Adams

Social Work and Mental Handicap
David Anderson

Beyond Casework
James G. Barber

Social Work with Addictions
James G. Barber

Citizen Involvement
Peter Beresford and Suzy Croft

Practising Social Work Law
Suzy Braye and Michael Preston-Shoot

Social Workers at Risk
Robert Brown, Stanley Bute and Peter Ford

Social Workers and Mental Illness
Alan Butler and Colin Pritchard

Social Work and Europe
Crescy Cannan, Lynn Berry and Karen Lyons

Residential Work
Roger Clough

Social Work and Child Abuse
David M. Cooper and David Ball

Management in Social Work
Veronica Coulshed

Social Work Practice
Veronica Coulshed

Social Work and Local Politics
Paul Daniel and John Wheeler

Sociology in Social Work Practice
Peter R. Day

Anti-Racist Social Work
Lena Dominelli

Working with Abused Children
Delia Doyle

Evaluating for Good Practice
Angela Everitt and Pauline Hardiker

Applied Research for Better Practice
Angela Everitt, Pauline Hardiker, Jane Littlewood and Audrey Mullender

Student Supervision in Social Work
Kathy Ford and Alan Jones

Working with Rural Communities
David Francis and Paul Henderson

Children, their Families and the Law
Michael D.A. Freeman

Family Work with Elderly People
Alison Froggatt

Child Sexual Abuse
Danya Glaser and Stephen Frosh

Computers in Social Work
Bryan Glastonbury

Working with Families
Gill Gorell Barnes

Women, Management and Care
Cordelia Grimwood and Ruth Popplestone

Women and Social Work
Jalna Hanmer and Daphne Statham

Youth Work
Tony Jeffs and Mark Smith (eds)

Problems of Childhood and Adolescence
Michael Kerfoot and Alan Butler

Communication in Social Work
Joyce Lishman

Working with Violence
Carol Lupton and Terry Gillespie (eds)

Social Work with Old People
Mary Marshall

Applied Psychology for Social Workers
Paula Nicolson and Rowan Bayne

Crisis Intervention in Social Services
Kieran O'Hagan

Social Work with Disabled People
Michael Oliver

Care Management
Joan Orme and Bryan Glastonbury

Social Care in the Community
Malcolm Payne

Working in Teams
Malcolm Payne

Working with Young Offenders
John Pitts

Effective Groupwork
Michael Preston-Shoot

Effective Probation Practice
Peter Raynor, David Smith and Maurice Vanstone

Practice Learning and Teaching
Steven Shardlow and Mark Doel

Social Work with the Dying and Bereaved
Carole R. Smith

Child Care and the Courts
Carole R. Smith, Mary T. Lane and Terry Walsh

Criminology for Social Work
David Smith

Social Work and Housing
Gill Stewart and John Stewart

Focus on Families
Christine Stones

Anti-Discriminatory Practice
Neil Thompson

Dealing with Stress
Neil Thompson, Michael Murphy and Steve Stradling

Working with Mental Illness
Derek Tilbury

Community Work
Alan Twelvetrees

Social Work and Empowerment

Robert Adams

MACMILLAN

© British Association of Social Workers 1990, 1996

First edition published as *Self-Help, Social Work and Empowerment* 1990
Reprinted 1993

This edition published as *Social Work and Empowerment* 1996 by
MACMILLAN PRESS LTD
Houndmills, Basingstoke, Hampshire RG21 6XS
and London
Companies and representatives
throughout the world

ISBN 0—333—65809—4

A catalogue record for this book is available from the British Library.

10   9   8   7   6   5   4   3   2   1
05   04   03   02   01   00   99   98   97   96

Printed in Malaysia

Series Standing Order (Practical Social Work)

If you would like to receive future titles in this series as they are published, you can make use of our standing order facility. To place a standing order please contact your bookseller or, in case of difficulty, write to us at the address below with your name and address and the name of the series. Please state with which title you wish to begin your standing order. (If you live outside the UK we may not have the rights for your area, in which case we will forward your order to the publisher concerned.)

Standing Order Service, Macmillan Distribution Ltd,
Houndmills, Basingstoke, Hampshire, RG21 6XS, England.

To Winifred Adams

Contents

List of Figures

Preface to the First Edition

This book grew partly from personal experiences of the need for self-help to contribute to the care of my own relatives and partly from my efforts to support the self-help initiatives of MIND, as the then chairperson of MIND's advisory committee in Yorkshire and Humberside. To that chance initiation into the politics of empowerment in mental health I owe a debt to Norman Jepson and John Crowley. Through involvement in Mind Your Self in Leeds, my collaboration with Gael Lindenfield, who founded it, led to several books and other publications. The book began partly also with the awareness that despite the growing numbers of handbooks on self-help, there was a need for an accessible yet critical text, which would provide a framework for the development of more effective relationships between professionals and self-helpers.

Several years later, during study leave from the College, I started to write on the basis of a series of visits to a wide variety of self-help groups and organisations throughout the UK. I should like to record my appreciation to the many people to whom, in the process, I spoke about the subject matter of this book. The list is too long to mention everyone here, but thanks are due in any case to Helen Allison, Mike Archer, Don Barton, David Brandon, Francis Conway, Gilly Craddock, Dave Crenson, Parul Desai, Nick Ellerby, John Errington, Alec Gosling, John Hannan, Gerry Lynch, Peter McGavin, Sam McTaggart, Jim Pearson, Tom Rhodenberg, Alan Robinson, Gill Thorpe, Bob Welburn and Tom Woolley. I am particularly grateful also to Dorothy Whitaker and Terence O'Sullivan for their comments on earlier drafts of this book, and to Paddy Hall for his ideas on community education.

Part of the process of production has been based at home, I have to acknowledge that my own household has seen its share of debates about self-help and empowerment over the past eighteen months and many improvements to the text have resulted from these. So, particular thanks are due to Pat, Charlotte, Kirsty, Jade and George.

Finally, I am learning as I write how valuable is the guidance and support of a good editor. For her encouragement and patience at the critical stages, my thanks go to Jo Campling.

It goes without saying, but needs saying of course, that, whilst much of the content of the book reflects the various contributions of those mentioned, among many others, all the opinions expressed in it, and any errors, are entirely my own.

ROBERT ADAMS

Preface to the Second Edition

I welcome the opportunity to update this book, because, since it was written in 1988, the concept of self-help has been largely overshadowed in social work by that of empowerment. This is not to say that self-help has disappeared, but that whereas self-help was the fashionable term of the 1980s, as indeed it was of the same decade a century earlier, a quite remarkable conjunction of concepts at the turn of the decade has led to the widespread adoption by the social work field of the term 'empowerment'. But I argue in this book that it is dangerous to assume that practice is enhanced, and people's interests advanced, simply by tacking a few paragraphs on empowerment on to circulars, procedures and guidelines as they stand. The rigorous application of empowerment to social work theory and practice requires the reappraisal of the status quo rather than the bolting on of another novelty. The two dimensions brought to bear in the framework for empowering social work in this book – the different levels of empowering practice and reflective practice – synthesise to offer *empowerment-in-practice* as one expression of what I believe is now the dominant paradigm in social work, replacing the paradigm of client treatment which dominated social work in former decades. I locate this shift in its wider context in a forthcoming book: *The Personal Social Services: Clients, Consumers or Citizens?*, listed in the Bibliography. The working-out of the application of empowerment-in-practice to the many different areas of social work involves theorising in and about practice. With some exceptions, dealt with mainly in Chapter 4, it will necessitate the overhaul of virtually all the social work literature – clearly a task far beyond the scope of this second edition of an existing book on empowerment and self-help in social work in Britain. To give an example, however, the framework set out in this book challenges the thrust of consumerist, managerially led, technically driven (rather than inspired from professional practice) context in which social work takes place. At a more mundane level, the fact that this is a book on empowering, written *for* the social work field, *about* empowering service users is, to say the least, paradoxical, is probably patronising and on occasions downright oppressive. However, the development of an empowering practice in social work is a professional necessity, which entails taking on board the complexities and ambiguities of the paradigm of empowerment as well as its obvious applications, aspects of which are examined chapter by chapter as follows:

Chapter 1 discusses the meanings which may be associated with the problematic concept of empowerment. Chapter 2 explains what is meant by a paradigm shift and develops a framework for empowerment-in-practice. Chapter 3 examines the basis for empowerment through reflective practice. Chapter 4 teases out those aspects of work with individuals, which are more amenable to empowerment. Chapters 5 and 6 deal with empowering work with groups and Chapter 7 with empowerment as it applies in community groups and organisations. Chapter 8 tackles the implications of the paradigm of empowerment for evaluation and research. Chapter 9 examines the problematic features of relations between social workers and service users inherent in the tension between accountable work and empowerment-in-practice. Chapter 10 draws some general conclusions about the issues raised by empowering social work, for individual practitioners and for the teams and organisations in which they work.

My thanks are due to Dr Raymond Jack and Jane Thompson for reading and commenting on an earlier draft of this new edition.

ROBERT ADAMS

List of Abbreviations

AA	Alcoholics Anonymous
ACC	Association of County Councils
Al-Anon	Organisation for relatives and friends of peopl with a drink problem
AMA	Association of Metropolitan Authorities
ARC	Asian Resource Centre, Birmingham
BASW	British Association of Social Workers
CARE	Cancer Aftercare and Rehabilitation Society
CCETSW	Central Council for Education and Training in Social Work
CVS	Council for Voluntary Service
CR	Consciousness-raising
DH	Department of Health
DHSS	Department of Health and Social Security
GMHC	Gay Men's Health Crisis
HIV/AIDS	Humano Immune Virus/Acquired Immune-deficiency Syndrome
NCVO	National Council for Voluntary Organisations
PSHPG	Peer Self-help Psychotherapy Groups
SCF	Save the Children Fund
THT	Terrence Higgins Trust
WHO	World Health Organisation

1

Concept of Empowerment

Introduction

This chapter explores the meaning of the term 'empowerment', examining its relationship with neighbouring concepts such as self-help and user-led activities. In the process, the intrinsically problematic features of ideas about empowerment are highlighted. This leads to the conclusion that it is more realistic to talk about versions of empowerment, rather than about a unitary and unambiguous concept.

Growing significance of empowerment

Empowerment is a term which only a few years ago hardly received a mention in standard British social work texts (see, for example, Coulshed, 1991). But in the 1990s it has achieved prominence. There has been a spate of publications, which inspire confidence since they indicate the willingness of researchers, policymakers and practitioners to apply the notion of empowerment to different aspects of the human services (see, for example, Adams, 1991, 1994; Braye and Preston-Shoot, 1995; Green, 1991; Holdsworth, 1991; Shor, 1992; Sleeter, 1991; Stewart, 1994; Wolfendale, 1992; Clarke and Stewart, 1992). At the same time, the application of the word 'empowerment' to different areas of theory, policy and practice brings with it dangers: the concept may be diluted, distorted, exploited as a topic by researchers or students, or colonised by one interest group, such as community care managers or practitioners rather than service users And

1

carers. One difficulty with empowerment as an idea is that it has been linked with intrinsically problematic, though desirable, fatures of social work, such as anti-oppressive practice. It is no exaggeration to state that the growing currency of the concept of empowerment makes it necessary to review critically, and possibly reinterpret and revise, much of the social work literature as quickly as possible. This should advance anti-oppressive practice, perhaps by taking on board the liberating potential of the framework set out in Chapter 2 for empowerment-in-practice, as a means of empowering both service users and social workers.

Yet whilst, as I noted in the first edition of this book, 'empowerment has come of age in the late 1980s', Karen Baistow (Baistow, 1994) rightly concludes that it has yet to achieve maturity, either as a critically understood concept, or as reflective practice. This is not surprising, given its significance for social work in particular and in the human services in general. For empowerment is not simply an elaboration of any single existing social work method, though it can be shown to have links with all of them. It is not derived exclusively from individually-based, person-centred or problem-focused, social or environmental approaches to social work. The antecedents to empowerment are a combination of traditions of mutual aid, self-help and, more recently, movements of liberation, rights and social activism, strengthened by anti-racism, feminism, critiques of inequalities and oppressions arising from social class, age, disability, sexuality, religion and other differences. It relates closely to movements for users' rights and user participation, though it should not be regarded necessarily as a means of bridging the gaps between providers and users of services (The User-Centred Services Group, 1993). Such activities, including partnerships between users and workers, actually may inhibit or contradict empowerment.

Despite these cautions, empowerment in all domains and sectors of practice could be, if it has not already become, *the* central, energising feature of social work. It is central to social work theory and practice. It has a legitimate place in all aspects of social work. In many situations, without empowerment, it could be argued that something fundamental is missing from the social work being practised.

A transcendent paradigm

The 1980s was the decade when social work lost ground against Thatcherite individualism and assaults on its credibility through various scandals and inquiries. In the 1990s, consumerism came to dominate the newly created managed quasi-markets for the delivery of health and social care services. Empowerment has to be seen as a means of transcending these social and political limitations and liberating both workers and service users. But it could also be regarded as a rhetorical gesture, a device of government to keep the consumers of welfare in their places in the queues for dole, social security, private health and welfare, and national lottery prizes. According to Mullender and Ward, empowerment is a term 'used to justify propositions which, at root, represent varying ideological and political positions', and which 'lacks specificity and glosses over significant differences'. It 'acts as a "social aerosol", covering up the disturbing smell of conflict and conceptual division' (1991, p.1). This book explores the ambiguities inherent in these alternative standpoints.

An empowering practice needs to be purposeful. This book sets out to provide social workers with a frame work for that purposeful practice. It provides a basis for competence in dealing with the field of empowerment, assuming that competence in practice rests on a combination of critical understanding, knowledge and skills in an appropriate context of values. In tackling this, the first task is to clarify the concept of empowerment and to relate it to other allied concepts such as self-help, before examining in more detail the nature of the work involved.

Scope of empowerment: theory and method

What is empowerment? Empowerment literally means 'becoming powerful' but in social work it has come to mean much more than that. It embraces both theory and method. The *Dictionary of Social Work* defines empowerment theory as 'theory concerned with how people may gain collective control over their lives, so as to achieve their interests as a group, and a method by which social workers seek to enhance the power of people who lack it' (Thomas and Pierson, 1995, p. 134). The dictionary definition links empowerment with self-help: 'Empowerment can refer to user participation in services and to the self-help movement generally, in which groups take action on their own behalf, either in cooperation with, or independently of, the statutory services' (Thomas and Pierson, 1995, pp. 134–5).

Empowerment inevitably is a political concept, though the extent to which this is apparent to those involved depends on their approach and the circumstances in which empowering work takes place. The political dimension of the concept of empowerment is not party political, in that its activist tone transcends party politics; it is not a legal term (such as community service, intermediate treatment, and so on) derived from the law; it is a concept which, despite the risks charted in Chapter 9, is rapidly being colonised by professionals, but not yet so as to marginalise or exclude service users; it is a generic concept, which can be attached to any aspect of practice. Its adoption by service users and activists in such areas as disability, mental health and anti-racist and anti-sexist practice, gives it resonance with radical rather than traditional practice. The main focus of this book is on enabling people to develop an empowering social work. 'Empowering practice, like the demands of the user movements it serves, seeks change not only through *winning power* – bringing to those who have been oppressed the exercise of control over what happens to them – but through transforming it' (Mullender and Ward, 1991, p. 6).

Concepts associated with empowerment

Empowerment may be defined as the means by which individuals, groups and/or communities become able to take control of their circumstances and achieve their own goals, thereby being able to work towards helping themselves and others to maximise the quality of their lives. Associated with this general statement, we can distinguish a number of major concepts, as follows:

Democratisation

Among the best known exponents in Britain of empowerment as a democratising process, are Beresford and Croft. Their two studies which have contributed most to this area are the study of a patch-based approach to delivering welfare services (Beresford and Croft, 1986) and the research into citizen involvement funded by the Joseph Rowntree Foundation (Beresford and Croft, 1993). The latter research illustrates the barriers to participation – progress towards which is an uphill struggle. On another tack, Sainsbury has written of the need not to create a false dichotomy between the roles of social work in furthering participation *by* people and those of protection *of* people, both of which are necessary in social work. He cautions against unrealistically anticipating that social work will be able to fight effectively against the tendency of society to promote differences between people in terms of income and power. He notes that this may be unattainable at present, since it is only possible to pursue social justice through achieving equality if citizens' social rights are equated with systems for allocating resources based on principles of social justice (Sainsbury, 1989, pp. 105–6).

Advocacy and self-advocacy

All aspects of advocacy and self-advocacy are potentially empowering. Advocacy and empowerment co-exist in many forms. Advocacy is the activity of negotiating or representing on behalf of a person. Payne distinguishes case advocacy, by which the worker seeks to enhance people's access to services, from cause advocacy, which seeks to promote social change for social groups from which these people come (Payne, 1991, p. 225). The roots of self-advocacy are generally regarded as being in the concept of advocacy in the area of learning disability, known at the time as 'mental handicap' (Lawson, 1991, p. 70). Self-advocacy is the process of the person representing herself or himself. Collective self-advocacy involves activity by groups of people on their own behalf (see Chapter 4).

Normalisation/social role valorisation

These concepts refer to processes by which disabled people and people with mental health problems have engaged in movements towards them maintaining and promoting their own independence and managing their own lives (Wolfensberger, 1972; Towell, 1988; Sinclair, 1988 quoted in Payne, 1991, p. 226).

Consciousness-raising

Although empowerment does not always figure explicitly in the literature concerning consciousness-raising, it is implicit in the process. One illustration of this is the women's therapy movement, based upon groups, involving individuals benefiting therapeutically but also gaining awareness of the social context of their problems and developing ways of addressing these. Women's therapy groups are described more fully in Chapter 5. Another illustration is through community work, which despite its difficult history in local authority-funded practice since the mid-1970s, as we shall see in Chapter 7 is a presence in the 1990s (Jacobs and Popple, 1994).

User-led practice

A range of approaches, both traditional and new, conservative and radical, come under this heading. From the 1970s, there has been a trend towards people in receipt of welfare benefits and health and personal social services demanding more control over the services provided for them. As Craig notes, this is located in the wider context of community action by poorer people (Craig, 1989) and the gap between the encouragement by government of participation by service users on the one hand and the lack of resources to underpin such participation on the other (Craig, 1992). Undoubtedly, taking the initiative by engaging in user-led activities is one route to self-empowerment and the empowerment of others. But it is necessary to distinguish the objective judgement that one person may make about another person necessarily being empowered, because of involvement in a user-group, and the subjective experience of that person. For example, the children and young people who receive the magazine *Who Cares?*, which states it is produced 'for young people in the care system', are taking part in an initiative *by* children and young people. But this involvement may occur at different levels. An individual may pick up a copy of the magazine and scan through it, before asking another person to help with reading its contents, contribute a letter or article, or be part of a local *Who Cares* group. At one extreme an individual may do none of these things yet feel empowered. At the other, she or he may continue to be a leading member of a local *Who Cares* group, precisely *because of* a feeling of being disempowered.

Radical social work

It is difficult to establish the relationship between empowerment and other concepts, such as those rooted in a range of radical ideas. Radicalism is a generic term for a wide range of standpoints, of which space only allows a brief mention here.

Marxist socialist perspectives generally seek empowerment as a means of promoting contradictions in society, with a view to eventually achieving change (Payne, 1991, p. 225). Rojek (1986) argues that advocacy and empowerment have their origins in fundamentally different objectives from the Marxist and radical perspectives to which they are closely related. Empowerment and advocacy are rationalist; that is, they have links with humanist and existential theory and practice in that they emphasise self-knowledge and self-control, accepting that people can control their own lives by rational, cognitive means (Payne, 1991, p. 227); they also assume that the environment can be changed directly, in favour of the service user. One immediate consequence of the rationalist basis for empowerment approaches is that failure to achieve immediate major changes in the conditions of their lives is likely to make people feel disappointed and therefore disillusioned with empowerment. Adherents to radical social work have propounded empowerment. One version of collective action in practice is linked with a more explicitly socialist agenda, such as the Marxist view expounded by Walker and Beaumont in the closing pages of their book (Walker and Beaumont, 1981, pp. 174–95). This radical critique of probation work, which relies heavily on social and environmental explanations of people's problems, is an alternative to those which are individually based (Walker and Beaumont, 1981, pp. 89–93). Thompson locates empowerment exclusively in the arena of radical social work, which he describes as

> an approach to social work which seeks to locate the problems experienced by clients in the wider social context of structured inequalities, poverty, inadequate amenities, discrimination and oppression. It sees social work as primarily a political venture, a *struggle* to humanise, as far as possible the oppressive circumstances to which clients are subject. It is premised on the key notion of *empowerment*, the process of giving greater power to clients in whatever ways possible – resources, education, political and self-awareness and so on. (Thompson, 1993, p. 32)

This extract glosses over the inherent paradox of professional involvement in empowerment, which revolves round the desirability of professionals *giving* power to other people.

Anti-oppressive practice

Critiques of oppression from Black perspectives (see the discussion of the work of Solomon, 1976, quoted in Payne, 1991, pp. 228–32), feminism, campaigns against ageism and the disability movement, have all converged on the concept of, and need for empowerment. This growing body of literature on anti-oppressive practice in social work has been responsible, more than any other factor, for enhancing the significance of the paradigm of empowering social work. Empowerment is anti-oppressive, as Ward and Mullender rightly observe (Ward and Mullender, 1991), though we should exercise caution about claiming that user-directed groups, no matter how empowered, will change the structural features of the world in which members live (Page, 1992).

Post-modernism and social work in the New Age

Perhaps historians will look back from the early years of the twenty-first century and identify the creation of managed markets in health and social care in the early 1990s as an early confirmation by government of the post-modern fragmentation of New Age social work. The wider changes which have produced the fragmentation of socialist movements, of which the changing political complexion of European countries affected by the disappearance of the 'Iron Curtain' is one manifestation, can be linked with the dissolution during the latter part of the twentieth century in many countries of the dichotomy between the single political options of Left and Right. The post-modern era, some commentators claim, provides opportunities for a politics which transcends the grand theories, such as those of Marx, and gives space to a multiplicity of diverse voices. The fragmentation of the personal social services into many small providers could be seen as one manifestation of the disaggregation of the large monopolistic local authority providers.

Ironically, just as in the mixed economy of care, some aspects of provision, such as quality assurance (Adams, *Quality Social Work*, forthcoming) are being directed more closely than hitherto by central government through bodies such as the Social Services Inspectorate and the Audit Commission, so in social work theory and practice the term 'anti-oppressive work' has provided a language for the paradigm of empowerment, which transcends the policies and politics of the many different groups and interests involved in social work. In the post-modern era, empowerment and anti-oppressive work have the potential either to become the new unifying, or divisive, themes of social work.

Empowerment: as essentially contested concept in social work

Empowerment is a tricky concept to handle, partly because it is inherently problematic, partly because of contextual factors in its use. The inherently problematic nature of empowerment is part of a wider pattern of insecurity and instability in social work as a minor profession, drawn attention to by Schon (1991, p. 23). Neither the client treatment paradigm, nor the empowerment paradigm which replaced it, contribute to a knowledge base which is systematically developed, scientifically proven and part of a public and professional consensus about the values, techniques and skills to be adopted by qualified and practising social workers. Within the paradigm of empowerment-in-practice, the concept of power is essentially contested. This could be represented in the critical perspective of post-modernism on its major predecessor theories which attempted to impose grand theories on the understanding of people and societies (see Figure 2.2

in Chapter 2). In this light, the focus on empowerment reinforces the centrality of power embedded in masculine-dominated knowledges of sociology in general and, for example, Marxist theory in particular (Adams, 1991; Adams, 1992; Adams, 1994, pp. 235–6). Thus, of protests by young people in schools, it has been nóted that 'there is a tension, not just between interpretations but between the knowledges which inform them. The struggles of young people to assert their critiques of schooling since the mid-1970s can be allied with those of feminist and environmentalist critiques of "domination" as a tenet of the masculine conceptualizations of the knowledges employed to frame sociological theories' (Adams, 1991, pp. 177–8). Again, the histories of

post-rehabilitation riots provide the stimulus to deconstruct the universalist assumptions of the Marxist analysis which in various forms sustained their predecessors during the consciousness-raising period. One outcome of this deconstruction may be what Rutherford calls a cultural politics of difference (Rutherford, 1990). Thus, whilst research has accurately identified issues such as long-term imprisonment (Scraton *et al.*, 1991) as central to the explanation of protests by prisoners in the latter quarter of the twentieth century, it is crucial that this factor does not dominate and exclude from consideration any experience of imprisonment which offers the setting for political antagonism between the authorities and prisoners. The fragmented character of incidents points to the need to transcend the former globalized unities sought by rioters without replicating them. Post-rehabilitation riots put onto the agenda of discourse about penality the diversity of prisoners and the issues of imprisonment. They offer the opportunity of responding to riots in ways which transcend and transform the dominant values of hierarchy, militarism, machismo, oppression and violence in the prison systems of Britain and the US, 'not attempting to construct oppositions based on hierarchies of value and power, not through the politics of polarity, but in the recognition of the otherness of ourselves, through the transformation of the relations of subordination and discrimination' (Rutherford, 1990, p. 26). The task is to move beyond the multi-faceted oppressions replicated in repeated riots to an explanation of their politics which enables their differences to be reconciled, without containing them in false unity. (Adams, 1994, pp. 235–6)

These extracts imply a need to view hesitantly totalising frameworks for the concept of empowerment and any attempt to construct a global framework for the application of empowerment to practice. Further, they lay a basis for the critique of dominant knowledges of professional practice, embodied in the more tentative, and anti-oppressive framework for empowerment-in-practice, developed in Chapter 2 (see Figure 2.1).

Some risks associated with empowerment-in-practice

Paradox of empowering without doing people's empowering for them

There is a need to move beyond the perception of empowering as something which is done to you, or which you do to yourself, and then pass on to someone else. There is a risk that a book about empowering work will slip into the assumption that it is largely or wholly professionals who empower other people, such as service users. Associated with this is a range of means (see Chapter 9 for examination of these) by which professionals may invade the territory of service users and reduce their scope for self-empowerment.

One person's empowerment may be another person's disempowerment

The process of empowerment operates at the levels of the individual, group, family, organisation and community, and also in the different sectors of people's lives. One person may feel empowered because of something realised or understood, another may experience empowerment once a new job, course or career opportunity is achieved.

Danger of dilution: from empowerment to enablement

By the nature of the popularity of the concept of empowerment, there is a danger of attaching it to social work activities in an inappropriate way and also of reducing its scope and also its power to improve people's circumstances. For instance, the cutting edge of the concept of empowerment is blunted by the tendency to speak as though it is merely another form of *enabling* act by professionals.

Dangers of addressing too many target groups and speaking to none adequately

Empowerment may also be applied not only to clients as self-helpers but also to social workers themselves. Whilst intrinsically valid, this may deflect attention away from the clients who should be the main focus of empowerment activities. It also may lead to the discussion of empowerment losing its sharpness and relevance to particular interests and groups engaged in the social work process.

Ambiguous relationship between self-help and empowerment

Self-help and empowerment have been co-opted by two interests which are fundamentally opposed to each other: right-wing consumerism and the movement for democratic control by users. Consequently, at the heart of the concepts of self-help and empowerment lies the ambiguity inherent in their embodying both individualist and collectivist ideologies.

The New Right advocates the right of people who can afford it to choose the goods and services they purchase, as consumers of welfare. Naturally, services only exist where it is economic for providers to make them available. Consumers of welfare in rural areas, poor people who cannot afford to pay, have more restricted choices than those who are better off, or those whose mobility and access is limited, and who consequently have no choice at all. On the other hand, there are movements for user control over the standards of services as well as the nature of services themselves.

There is a tendency for the social worker to view self-help as simply nothing to do with social work at all; or, self-help becomes a political football, kicked about by opposing political factions, regarded from the Left as a justification for cuts in the health and social services and from the Right as the route to prosperity.

The difficulty is that at first sight the two areas of self-help and social work seem to be incompatible. To caricature the position, socialist social workers may tend to dismiss self-help as a potentially destructive irrelevance while the more conservative use it is as an excuse for opting out. Either way, the territory of self-help activities gets less attention from social workers than it deserves. The relationship between self-help and empowerment-in-practice is close, since through self-help by service users, social workers and self-helpers can empower others and be empowered themselves.

Co-option of radical empowerment by the Right: consumerism versus participation

The area of empowerment is to some extent colonised by right-wing ideologies, policies and practices. This can be seen most obviously in community care, where the consumerist thrust of government policies is reflected, for example, in advice from the Social Services Inspectorate on how to work with service users. There are tensions between consumerist and participative approaches to community care. The consumerist approach to services – competitive tendering and contracting out – has been imported from the world of business into managed or quasi-markets in community care, in the health and social work/social services field. Consumerism has been increasingly adopted by the public sector since the early 1980s. Participative approaches have been associated with a critique of the lack of genuine user participation and democratisation of the provision and delivery of services and are exemplified by challenges from the disabled movement to the dominant consumerist ideology of service provision (Croft and Beresford, 1989).

Roots of empowerment lie partly in self-help

Part of the difficulty with the empowerment paradigm is that its contemporary forms have fed off anti-sexist, anti-racist, anti-disablist and other critical, anti-oppressive movements, whereas its historical roots lie partly in traditions of mid-Victorian self-help which tend to reflect the dominant values of society at that time. Whereas in theory, self-help is a neutral concept, in practice in the nineteenth century it was wielded by the prosperous middle classes to extol their own virtues. In contrast, empowerment, in professional social work discourse, is oriented towards personal and social change in pursuit of anti-oppressive values and, therefore, its practitioners are more likely than their Victorian ancestors in self-help, to work in alliance with undervalued people in society. However, self-help has not only been associated with reactionary politics and policies. In the second half of the twentieth century, some radical practice referred back, not to its individualistic self-interest, but to its roots in mutual aid, exemplified in the friendly society movement from the eighteenth century. Whilst in formal terms, radical empowerment as a concept was imported into Britain in the late 1980s, it relates to long-established radical aspects of the traditions of self-help and mutual aid, one expression of which in Britain are the friendly societies and credit unions for mutual aid in saving and insurance. Payne quotes the use of the concept in a publication in the USA in 1982 whilst Mullender and Ward refer to its use in a publication as long ago as 1977 (Mullender and Ward, 1991, pp. 33 and 183).

Concept of self-help: fuelling empowerment practice

Self-help is the most significant traditional activity in Britain, on which empowerment practice draws. It has been much maligned since the 1970s. This is not to say that mid-Victorian self-help did not have its critics before then, but that aspects of the history of self-help – its middle class self-interested individualism rather than the less visible, but potentially more radical belief in the virtues of mutual aid – was the target of critical attention from the 1970s onwards.

The Conservative Government which came into power in 1979 took up a 'pull yourself up by your bootstraps' version of self-help; however, as noted above, the concept retained some currency with socialists and social democrats as mutual aid. Thus, in the 1980s, for example, credit unions began to spread, as, apart from anything else, some community groups realised their potential for linking personal support and community development.

Self-help is a broad-based social movement both in Britain and the USA, with its roots in the mainstream of pragmatic thinking. Self-help may be defined as a process, group or organisation comprising people coming together or sharing an experience or problem, with a view to individual and/or mutual benefit. Self-help may thus be viewed as one form of empowerment. Self-help illustrates a particular strain of anti-intellectualism, which in Britain is exemplified in a mixture of utilitarian philosophy and preference for amateurism and charitable giving over professionalism embedded in theory and the social sciences, which besets present-day social work education, training and practice. Insofar as self-help is still heir to a well-entrenched tradition of amateurism and voluntary effort, links can be made with the British context of mid-Victorian philanthropy in which self-help was first associated, through the Charity Organisation Society.

In health and social care, several social and economic factors may have been associated with the growth and spread of self-help. These include the impulse towards decarceration, the contraction of medical and clinical practice and a degree of disillusionment with this, the growth of alternative practice and finally the heightened awareness of some service users beyond their situation as stigmatised clients. Further, within social work there has been a tendency since the 1960s for professional power to be viewed more critically, allied with the very distinct but perhaps convergent impulse of social workers towards harnessing the positive influence of networks of consumers of social services in helping activities of many kinds in the community.

The traditions of self-help and mutual aid

Political judgements made by commentators about what sort of health and social work services are desirable affect their views about self-help itself. To one person, it may be seen as a highly attractive option, whilst to another it represents an unattractive consequence of the contracting Welfare State. At one extreme, it appears ideal, at the other extreme, it may represent anathema.

This was true in the past also. Samuel Smiles, writing in mid-Victorian England, saw self-help as an expression of individualism, since it denotes activities whereby individuals and small groups deal with their problems (Smiles, 1890). The role of professionals is largely limited to exhorting people to pull themselves up by their own bootstraps, with a little materials and spiritual support for those whose efforts prove they deserve it. In contrast, Kropotkin (1902) writing before the Russian Revolution, saw the collective benefits of self-help, the goal being a nationally healthy community, aiming to fulfil the individual and provide insurance against people's loss of control over their own lives by improving their participation in the local community. In addition, he felt that self-help should set out to improve the self-awareness of individuals.

In one sense, self-help has always been popular. As Tax has pointed out (Tax, 1976, p. 448), self-help and mutual aid are probably as old as the history of people living in communities. Yet, in Britain they are viewed by some people as one product of encouragement by the 1979 incoming Conservative Government, or as in import from the self-help boom in the USA, which has gathered pace over the past fifty years. More recently, while self-help groups may be seen simply as a perpetuation of long-established, or even prehistoric forms of mutual aid, it is more accurate perhaps to regard them as midway between such traditional 'folk' activities and fully professional services (Killilea, 1976, p. 47).

One reason that self-help attracts such criticism from left-wing politicians and others is that, in Britain at least, for 150 years or more it has often reflected the values of middle-class society. Just over a century ago, Samuel Smiles put forward an essentially *bourgeois* view. From his respectable middle-class position, he preached that 'poverty often purifies, and braces a man's morals' (Smiles, 1875, p. 361). The harmful vice of charity was expressed in mere giving, which contrasted with the more considered charity of useful philanthropy (Smiles, 1875, p. 324). Hard work provided the preferred route to overcoming poverty, through self-denial, thrift, individual self-improvement and self-denying economy: 'The spirit of self-help is the root of all genuine growth in the individual; and, exhibited in the lives of many, it constitutes the true source of national vigour and strength' (Smiles, 1890).

The positive aspect of these ideas is that self-help still has a place in the tradition of philanthropy and voluntary action in Britain and that the movement did not die with the end of the nineteenth century. The negative feature is the persistent tendency of individualism, which proposes self-help, in some key areas of community care for example, as a substitute for statutory services rather than as complementary with, or supplementary to, them.

Self-help and voluntary action

In the past half century, in Britain at least, self-help has gained from the increased strength of the voluntary movement. But it should be noted that although self-help often involves voluntary activity, it is not synonymous with the voluntary sector. The enthusiasm for the Welfare State after the 1940s did not see the demise of self-help. In fact, the 1950s witnessed the growth of many self-help and pressure groups. A significant report on the roles of volunteers at the end of the 1960s (Aves, 1969) strengthened the base of the voluntary sector, which still provides the support and encouragement for many self-help initiatives.

But although voluntarism was gaining in strength from the 1960s, it was a further decade before the Wolfenden Report (1978) set the tone for the renewed emphasis specifically on self-help which has gathered momentum in Britain since then. Wolfenden emphasised the significance of the voluntary sector in developing partnerships between individuals, informal networks of support, voluntary bodies and the statutory agencies.

Values of self-help

Whilst at first sight the dominant approach to self-help and mutual aid may seem to buttress an individualistic view of social policy and a right-wing political stance, in fact groups and organisations adopt and reflect a wide range of perspectives from reactionary to radical.

According to Gartner and Riessman (1977, pp. 13–14), the philosophy of self-help is 'much more activist, consumer centred, informal, open and inexpensive'. It emphasises non-professional themes: 'the concrete, the subjective, the experiential and the intuitive – in contrast to the professional emphasis on distance, perspective, reflection, systematic knowledge and understanding'. This clearcut division is not one many self-helpers would accept, since many are committed to the latter view. But it is worthwhile trying to set out areas of values shared by much of the self-help field. There are five recurrent themes: self-management; empowerment; anti-bureaucracy; co-operation; common experiences.

Self-management

This theme involves both an attachment to the desirability of small groups of people in face-to-face settings, or networks or postal contacts which can be managed from home, and the belief in problem management. In most self-help groups and organisations, there is a belief in the importance of participants having the skills to manage their own self-help, whether this be self- management, group leadership or whatever.

Empowerment through self-help

In fact, although in many countries people engaged in self-help would say they have been involved in empowering people for years, the actual term 'empowerment' is one which in Britain has been in widespread use only since the late 1980s. It is increasingly common for social workers to get involved in self-help activities who believe strongly in the principle of people moving towards improving their control over their circumstances.

Anti-bureaucracy

Self-help groups and organisations often assert the need to develop ways of organising themselves which are different from many of the organisations with which they have come into contact as clients. This frequently involves an emphasis on avoiding hierarchical and bureaucratic patterns of organisation.

Co-operation

The emphasis on mutual help or joint care (Wilson, 1988), which distinguishes much self-help activity from selfish individualism, is often expressed in a belief in democracy, equality of status and power within groups and organisations, shared leadership and co-operation in decision-making. Some self-help initiatives have much in common with co-operatives.

Common experiences

Quite often a requirement of participants is a willingness to start from the common base of experience defined by the group or organisation. This can involve members of a group necessarily sharing issues or problems. It also implies a resistance to internal divisions in groups between expert and lay members, therapists and clients. Although some self-help actually espouses anti-professionalism, this is not always the case. What is more often held to is the principle that the self-help process should not simply be the property of professionals but should be able to be initiated and engaged in by any of the participants. On the whole, research suggests that self-help groups tend to accept rather than reject relationships with professionals (Lieberman and Borman, 1976, p. 407), whilst at the same time self-help may involve a profound critique of professional activities (Gartner and Riessman, 1976, p. 12).

International developments in self-help

The influence of the US on self-help in Western Europe in fact may be no more significant than what has been learned from the developing countries, the illustration of Nijeri Kori in Chapter 4 representing this latter influence. The transnational nature of self-help cannot be ignored.

The mushrooming literature on self-help in the US, mirrored to a lesser extent in Britain, indicates a high level interest in both of these countries. But in Britain at any rate, this has not been accompanied by a similar enthusiasm for research (Richardson, 1983, p. 203). Again, some people have suggested that in the US and in Britain self-help is a middleclass phenomenon. Diversification of self-help can be demonstrated through the range of areas covered. Unell charts a variety of group initiatives concerned with different physical conditions and life crises (Unell, 1987, p. 30).

However, there is still little evidence of old people, for instance, taking self-help initiatives. Further, from Unell's admittedly small-scale survey of professionals' views, it is clear that many see activities as only of use to a limited number of people. There is some truth in the image of self-help groups as catering primarily for middle-class people whose problems do not in any case require professional support or intervention.

In Western Europe, there is evidence of growing interest in self-help. In the Netherlands, there are groups catering for such aspects as euthanasia, suicide, transvestism and sado-masochism (Bakker and Karel, 1983, p. 167). Many of these relate to wider political and social issues and are associated to a degree with increasing awareness of the limitations of statutory health, education and social welfare provisions. In Germany, the ecological, peace and women's movements give the impression of much activity in the self-help area. In Belgium, a lack of national funding beyond a few specialist projects contrasts with a growing provincial and local support for self-care and self- help (Branckaerts, 1983, p. 158). In France, the strength of private provision alongside public health and social services, and the unpopularity of voluntary action itself, apparently still leaves scope for self-help initiatives either as alternative to, or as compensation for, weaknesses in other sectors (Ferrand-Bechmann, 1983, p. 186).

In the developing countries, self-help and mutual aid commonly comprise the core not just of health and social services but also of the economic and social fabric itself. This applies from agriculture to education, from housing to the supply of energy. In most areas, the majority of the people since time immemorial have had to provide their own tools, buildings, skills and other resources, or run the risk of deprivation or death. The problems of Western industrial societies tend to arise from over-production and over-consumption, whereas in the Third World the reverse is true.

In the developing countries, self-help by poor people is as much a political issue as anywhere else. For instance, the shift to community-based, locally non-professionally led campaigns or programmes to change lifestyles, reduce environmental hazards or deal effectively with personal health and social problems, may involve confronting exploitive power in societies either apathetic, or actively hostile, towards any activity implying changes in their policies or practices. In many countries, self-help and self-care are much more of a substitute for non-existent health and social services than complementary with existing provision. Thus, between 65 per cent and 90 per cent of sick people in South and East Asia make use of self-administered herbal remedies (Stokes, 1981, p. 103). Again, research into leprosy in Chad indicates that traditional self-care is more effective than treatment by the medical services (Stokes, 1981, p. 104).

Self-help essentially operates as an alternative to, or a substitute for, social work. Much self-help activity, especially in groups, is referred to as user-led. User-led groups may be supportive of, indifferent towards, or critical of, social work. In the latter case, whether the user group is fairly long-lived or has a limited life, it tends to function as a critical presence in the field of helping services. That is, its presence generally implies criticism of existing services. This critical presence may be with regard to the practice of the individual social worker, the agency, the entire service, or indeed several services.

This brief review shows that the complex field empowerment in social work relates to many diverse, and to some extent problematic concepts and areas of practice. Not least, there is a divergence between contemporary anti-oppressive and equality-driven influences on empowerment and the traditions of self-help and mutual aid. Additionally, a critical understanding of empowerment needs to take account of the wider international context of the developing countries, as well as developments in Western Europe and the USA. In the next chapter, we consider the more immediate British context for the framework for empowerment developed there and used in the remainder of this book.

2

Framework for Empowerment-in-Practice

Introduction

We saw in the last chapter that although the concept of empowerment is rooted in a mixture of traditions of mutual aid and self-help as well as more recent liberation, rights and social activist movements, it offers social work the prospect of a different paradigm, rather than the adaptation or extension of an existing one. This chapter recognises that the contesting interpretations of empowerment create a variety of possible frameworks for developing practice. It takes account of the contextual factors shaping policies and practices with an empowerment dimension, including those factors which particularly affect the relationship between professionals and service users. The framework used here charts the level of empowerment against the degree of reflectiveness in practice. But its use in the remainder of this book is subject to the caution that there is no simple linear progression between the different levels of implementing empowerment. Also, the development of a reflective empowering practice involves recognising, specifying and addressing problematic features of situations, rather than adopting a quick-fix, technical problem-solving approach.

Contextual factors affecting empowerment

The fact that social workers have not related as effectively as they might have to the field of self-help and user-led practice contrasts with the massive amount of involvement which takes place in related, but quite distinct, areas; for instance, the widespread use of volunteers in social work has been noted (Holme and Maizels, 1978, p. 172). In contrast, seven main factors contribute to the relative neglect of user-led practice by social workers: demographic trends, social trends, constraints on social workers; social workers undervaluing the activities of service users; conceptual confusion about professional involvement; a lack of accessible demonstrations of effective practice; and last but not least, the underdevelopment of empowerment of service users and carers.

Demographic trends

Demographic and economic trends have a tremendous impact on the size and profile of the workloads of social services departments in general and social workers in particular. Rising unemployment, changes in technology and the economic recession in manufacturing have had harsher consequences for people who are unskilled, semi-skilled and unable but wanting to retrain, than for better qualified and relatively well-off people. Conditions of ethnic and cultural diversity in many parts of Britain still leave black people additionally disadvantaged. Women, people with disabilities or in other circumstances attracting social stigma, young, and inexperienced and older people, are likely to suffer difficulties. People in more than one of the above groups stand a still greater change of experiencing the inequalities of a divided society.

Increasing life expectancies and a rising divorce rate combine with changing pressures on, and earning and career opportunities for, women in a context where women's expectations are themselves changing. We may be witnessing not so much the decline of the family as a shift towards four-generational systems of caring in households, which produces ever-increasing burdens on a smaller-than-ever pool of available potential carers. In practical terms, this is the consequence of the demographic trends referred to above. In proportion to the number of dependants, children and older people in particular, the number of able-bodied adults is declining. Within this able-bodied group, the bulk of the task of looking after people in the community falls to female relatives.

Some groups, notably older people and people with disabilities, are particularly vulnerable to poverty, unemployment and a too restricted view of their own rights to qualify for help (Townsend, 1979). The workload of social workers has been affected also by the development of community care policies in work with elderly people, people with disabilities, people with mental illnesses and children and young people. The growing size of the elderly population, in absolute as well as relative terms, leads them to figure prominently as a client group. The increasing trends towards closing down large mental hospitals, hospitals for those with mental handicaps and community homes with education on the premises lead to questions being raised (Audit Commission, 1986) about whether adequate community-based services have been generated to replace them. The implementation of the NHS and Community Care Act 1990 saw the end of the virtual monopoly of social services departments over the provision of residential and day care services in these sectors. Private residential provision, registered but not necessarily quality-controlled by social services departments, subsequently was encouraged by the willingness of the DHSS to provide funding for residents. The creation of managed markets in the provision of health and social care amounted to the restructuring of the state response to people in need.

Social trends affect the focus of activity

The 1990s have seen massive shifts in the resourcing and administering, and consequent changes in the balance between statutory, voluntary and private provision, in the personal social services. The provision of personal social services, viewed through the prism of a post-modern perspective, may appear as many fragmented enterprises, dispersed in small units. In the wake of the NHS and Community Care Act 1990 there has been a striking diversification, even fragmentation, of providers of personal social services.

In contrast with such changes, arguments in favour of self-help alternatives to social work have been advanced for many years. More than twenty years ago, attention was drawn to the sociological notion of social networks as a non-casework means of supporting people who are isolated, elderly and with disabilities (Goldberg, 1966, p. 73). Administrative structures have certainly changed since that work was written, in a direction which reflects the growing size and strength of the voluntary sector, either independent of, or in partnership with, the statutory sector. The Griffiths Report (Griffiths, 1988, para 4.3–4, p. 7), publication of which was delayed by a government unsympathetic to its recommendations despite their consumerist tone, was eventually used as the basis for the NHS and Community Care Act 1990. Griffiths noted the importance of the voluntary, private and informal care sectors in providing community care and singled out the voluntary sector in many roles, including that of self-help (Griffiths, 1988, para 8.11, p. 26).

Great changes since the 1980s in the organisation and delivery of the personal social services, have been nowhere greater than in community care. The creation of internal markets in community care, through the NHS and Community Care Act 1990, has heralded a new relationship between the worker and the person receiving services. Thus in community care, the model of the professional treating the client's problems has been displaced largely by that of the service user choosing services as part of a care plan developed to meet individual needs. One of the signals of dramatic change is the increasing use of the term 'consumer' to describe the person receiving such services. Behind this term lie different perspectives – notably consumerist and participative (see Chapter 1) – on health and social care provision, which contribute to the context in which empowering work takes place.

The constraints on social workers affect the way they relate to service users

Far from the Seebohm Report (1968) heralding the end of the problems of organising social work, the professional autonomy of social workers continues to be compromised by their accountability to office managers who are separated from client-contact and motivated by bureaucratic rather than professional imperatives (Toren, 1972). Three trends in social work organisation have been identified: towards greater accountability, towards increasing decentralisation of government and localised delivery of services and towards reducing resources in real terms in relation to the tasks facing professional workers (Boateng, 1986, p. 3). In the face of these somewhat contradictory trends, the administration of social services departments has long been recognised as reinforcing accountability to the director rather than to the service user (Satyamurti, 1981). Social workers are often left to manage as best they can the inevitable tension between their statutory duty to supervise, inspect, to make independent recommendations or decisions and their accountability to the interests of service users, and to fight for more resources and for freedom to innovate. Since the mid-1980s these difficulties have been compounded by a number of scandals about poor practice, for example, in child protection – in Cleveland and the Orkneys – and residential child care – such as Pindown.

Social workers are gatekeepers of access to resources of support and help. They need to work within the compass of an ever-increasing and ever more complex legislative framework of statutory duties, combined with their growing role as child protection officers in the wake of child-abuse disclosures. This has had the effect of edging their long-term work with people to a lower priority than 'fire fighting' in areas such as child protection. Increasingly, in areas outside child care, social workers are thus under pressure to act as care managers rather than direct workers with service users – for example, as co-ordinators or enablers of care packages of private, voluntary and self-help.

The activities of service users are undervalued by some professionals

Social workers may claim that they are too busy to devise ways of working with users, that they have too little resources, that they are too preoccupied with 'essential' tasks. This may not be an intentional snub of the self-care sector, but an under-developed relationship with it often can be experienced as undervaluing users themselves. Research shows that education and training courses for professional social workers tend virtually to ignore the existence and potential of the entire voluntary sector (Gill and Andrews, 1987). The same is true for user-led practice. The question is, given the social and political trends, the resource constraints, the pressure on practice, how far can users contribute to giving consumers a better social work service and avoid becoming part of a cost-cutting confidence trick played on gullible practitioners and vulnerable consumers?

Conceptual confusion inhibits social work involvement in user-led practice

Social workers may shy away from user-led activity because the interests of users and social workers overlap, are distinct or mutually conflicting. Contradictions may arise from these complex relationships. For example, social care which involves negotiating and bringing helping resources to bear on a problem, may rule out user-led work.

How does a social worker get into user-led practice? Perhaps it is no fault of social workers that there is a lack of guidance on how to relate to people as empowered users rather than as disempowered clients. But the fact remains that despite the fact that many practitioners use the term 'empowerment' freely, rather less have developed concepts, let alone practices, which take them far into this field. Far too often, such work is seen as marginal to social work, whereas in fact instances can be found in the heartland of its territory.

Illustrations of proven effective practice are all too few

There is a dearth of examples of effective practice in self-help and empowerment. One area where there were initiatives in the 1970s and 1980s involved attempts to develop locally-based services, in a neighbourhood or patch. Research into attempts to implement different approaches to patch-based social work suggests that they may be hampered by three main problems: bureaucracy which works against local autonomy, views of professionalism which emphasise traditional approaches based on individual casework rather than more flexible and open-ended approaches, and finally, trade unionism which may restrict innovation through requiring detailed negotiations between management and unions before change can proceed (Hadley and McGrath, 1980, pp. 101–3). Even by its enthusiasts, the successful implementation of patch-based social services is said to depend on the commitment of managers and other staff, a significant allocation of training resources and the advice of an independent consultant (Hadley *et al.*, 1984, pp. 151–2). Although the advent of managed markets of purchase and provision in community care have occasioned a fundamental reorganisation of services in most areas which has consigned patch and neighbourhood approaches to history, one payoff was their legacy of models for service provision. Thus, for example, one view of an alternative organisation for social services provided by Hadley and Hatch (1981, p. 166), has the potential to empower service users, and embodies four principles: plural provision – a variety of community-based voluntary and informal as well as statutory services; decentralisation – the dominance of community-oriented provision; contractual and not hierarchical accountability; participation involving users and providers alongside each other in running local services.

Evidence of the lack of meaningful participation by people in the planning and delivery of social services can be gathered from a variety of sources (Beresford and Croft, 1981). Critics of patch schemes of social services provision argue that the advertised advantages such as increased mutual aid and self-help, public participation, democratisation and autonomy of local services, underplay shortcomings in their implementation (Beresford, undated). These criticisms raise questions about the involvement of the voluntary and informal sectors. Ironically, the attempt to decentralise services may sometimes achieve the opposite effect, with some aspects of management and service delivery, and the power accompanying them, being more centralised. In effect, this leads to tokenism rather than real democratisation. Also, the rhetoric about developing partnerships between statutory, voluntary and informal providers may thinly disguise the intention to cut the cost of services (Beresford, undated).

Consumerist and participative perspectives on service delivery, either of which may be adopted by service purchasers and providers, in the light of the NHS and Community Care Act 1990 necessitate the development of a framework for the use of empowerment in social work which is robust enough to address the issues of theory and practice, in the face of whichever of these perspectives is dominant in a given area of work. As we saw in Chapter 1, the dominance of consumerism is more of a threat to empowering practice than would the widespread adoption of an approach rooted in participative democracy.

Empowerment of service users and carers is underdeveloped

Although the paradigm of empowerment has emerged in Britain since the late 1980s, it was not until the requirements of qualified social workers published in Paper 30 was replaced in the review of the Dip. SW in 1994–95, that its currency was explicitly recognised by CCETSW (1991). Further, it is probably true to say that in Britain at any rate, its application in practice is relatively limited. In fact, there is lack of readily identifiable guidelines for practitioners and a tendency, as a result, for the term 'empowerment' to be used in a rather loose way. One danger of this is that its significance becomes lessened as its meaning is diluted. Empowerment may thus be used to mean simply 'enablement'. The account given of the 1989 BASW conference on empowerment (*Social Work Today*, 13 April 1989, p. 6) confirmed the need for the development of more coherent and positive strategies for empowering workers and service users. Whilst the comprehensive examination of empowerment is outside the scope of this book, the framework which follows is intended to further the development of empowerment in relation to social work.

Treatment and empowerment paradigms in social work

We noted in Chapter 1 that the roots of empowerment lie partly in traditions of self-help and mutual aid and partly in what may be viewed as the unprecedented consciousness raising and protest culture of the 1960s. But the character of empowerment in social work represents a paradigmatic change – revolution – rather than a gradual shift – evolution. This is justified by the inextricable embedding of the empowerment paradigm in anti-oppressive discourse. It makes necessary the re-interpretation of the entire literature of social work through the concept of empowerment. Empowerment offers a new approach or paradigm, rather than a modification of an existing one. It involves what Kuhn (1970) terms a paradigm shift. What do we mean by a paradigm shift?

Kuhn uses the term 'paradigm' to describe innovations which 'define the legitimate problems and methods of a research field for succeeding generations of practitioners'. They achieve this because they have two essential features. The innovation is 'sufficiently unprecedented to attract an enduring group of adherents away from competing modes of ... activity' and 'sufficiently open-ended to leave all sorts of problems for the redefined group of practitioners to resolve' (Kuhn, 1970, p. 10).

It is a strength from the point of view of this book, though some critics in the natural sciences would say a weakness of Kuhn's theory of how change occurs in a particular field, that a paradigm shift need not be based on a particular new piece of empirical research evidence coming to light. He was concerned, as a theoretical physicist, to understand how scientific advances took place and he realised the inadequacy of a history of science which assumes that each new empirical research finding puts a further brick in place in the process of constructing the wall of knowledge. He took an holistic view, based on evidence of the successive reconstructions of the way the world is understood. These often have been the outcome of controversy and conflict in science, over concepts which may derive in the first place from theoretical speculation or assertion, as much as from empirical observation. In other words, the interpretation of so-called factual evidence is shaped by the values of the researcher and by the historical and social context in which the research takes place.

Kuhn's ideas also may be criticised for portraying paradigms too much as self-contained, and producing a view of history as a series of more or less discrete happenings, with no necessary element of progress or evolution. But critics of the developmental assumptions which dominated social policy for many years would argue that social change should not be viewed as synonymous with progress. Kuhn has also been criticised for his argument that paradigms may exist at different levels of generality (Kuhn, 1970, p. 28). But it is important that he suggests also that differences may exist between the application of a paradigm in different fields. In other words, paradigms do not exist purely at the level of general, unchanging laws of nature. They may arise, and dominate, a particular area of professional activity, and within that area, specialists may produce their own, sometimes mutually conflicting versions of a particular paradigm.

Admittedly, there is a difficulty in distinguishing what Kuhn terms rules from paradigms (Kuhn, 1970, p. 43) and in working out how each applies to the field in question (Kuhn, 1970, p. 49). This is linked with the problem that Kuhn has conceptualised paradigms in a rather non-specific and open-ended way. This process involves developing guidance on the areas of practice most conducive to empowerment, and specifying how this may be furthered. As Kuhn notes, in the process, the paradigm itself may be refined (Kuhn, 1970, p. 34). Kuhn's refusal in these ways to adopt idealised accounts of the world or to retreat from the implications of his everyday observations of the ways researchers and practitioners actually act increase the relevance of his ideas to social work. His theory has the virtue that it reflects the complex realities not just of the world of research and practice in the natural sciences, but also in the social sciences, social policy and social work.

The essentially contested nature of the concepts of self-help and empowerment in social work is mirrored in Kuhn's comment that researchers and commentators may agree on the existence of a paradigm without reaching a consensus about its interpretation (Kuhn, 1970, p. 44). His suggestion that paradigms are simultaneously theoretical and experimental (Kuhn, 1972, p. 34) parallels the development of the literature in social work since the late 1980s, for instance, in the areas of anti-oppressive practice, reflective practice and empowerment. A number of conferences, conference papers, articles, papers, and one or two books, sometimes arising from research and sometimes written as textbooks, or from a practice base, have been influential in establishing empowerment by the mid-1990s as the dominant paradigm in social work. Even accepting that the route to practice development in social work differs significantly from that in the natural sciences, Kuhn's identification of the interdependence of theoretical and practice wisdom in that process crosses disciplinary boundaries, when he states that a 'a new theory is always announced together with applications . . . After it has been accepted, those same applications or others accompany the theory into the textbooks from which the future practitioner will learn his [*sic*] trade. They are not there merely as embroidery or even as documentation. On the contrary, the process of learning a theory depends on the study of applications . . .' (Kuhn, 1970, pp. 46–7). The development of the paradigm of empowerment and the working-out of its application to the many different areas of social work, are processes which are occurring simultaneously.

During the 1960s and 1970s, the treatment paradigm dominated social work. The word 'treatment' sometimes, but not invariably, meant the application of medical terminology of diagnosis and prescription. Even apart from this particular version of the treatment paradigm, the assumption was widespread that professionals knew best what would benefit people. It is difficult to be precise, because, as we saw in Chapter 1, the notion of self-help is inherently contradictory, but during the 1970s and 1980s self-help and user-led initiatives gained ground. By the mid-1990s, the empowerment paradigm was gaining ground. This involved the equation that effective social work was the product of social work work *with*, rather than *on*, people.

Though it involves a somewhat artificial simplification not reflected in the complex picture of practice, we can say that social work from the 1960s was concerned more with the treatment of clients whilst from the late 1980s it was concerned more with the empowerment of service users. The implications of this shift need teasing out in greater detail than we have space for here. But in summary, it is possible to see the replacement of casework and, at one extreme, the medical model of practice underpinned by psycho-social or psychoanalytic theories which dominated social work during the earlier period, with care packages and contractual agreements in social work with people, associated with theories – perhaps informed by one or more of feminism, Black liberation, social action, community work or radical politics – concerning empowerment of individuals, groups, organisations and communities. These theories gained ground during the

1970s and 1980s and had come of age by the early 1990s. The fact that commentators may disagree about the mapping of these shifts and all the detail involved, should not obscure the fundamental gulf between the client treatment paradigm and the service user empowerment paradigm.

Different ways of linking empowerment with practice development

Empowerment may be linked in different ways with practice development. None of these are mutually exclusive, but each has distinctive features: on a continuum (after O'Sullivan, 1994), as reflective practice (after Schon, 1991), as a ladder (after Arnstein, 1969), as a dialogic process (after Freire, originally published 1972/reprinted 1986), as a generic means of anti- oppressive practice (after Phillipson, 1992), or bringing together aspects of the work of Freire, Phillipson and Schon, in the framework set out below, for empowerment-in-practice.

Empowerment: on a continuum

O'Sullivan provides a typology of possibilities, on a horizontal axis or continuum: proposing that a continuum exists between total domination by the worker at one extreme and total control by the service user at the other. In between are various combinations, at a mid-point involving partnership between equal parties. To the extent that empowered people act autonomously while partners share power, entering into partnership may actually be experienced by some people as *disempowering.* The question arises as to whether there are points on the continuum where a conceptual break or qualitative gulf occurs, between two positions. O'Sullivan argues that such a gulf exists, between partnership, which may actually be disempowering for one of the partners, who may otherwise have been autonomous and empowered, and empowerment.

In one sense, to pontificate on an 'essentially correct' view is to replicate the oppressiveness against which empowering practice often struggles. A great variety of human experiences may be viewed as empowering. The liberated consciousness of Bonhoeffer writing in the condemned cell speaks to a view of mentally or spiritually based rather than materially-based empowerment; the writing of Marx emphasises changed material conditions as a precursor for empowerment; the framework set out below may involve either or both of these, or indeed a process which transcends not only dialectical materialism but all other conventional politics, in developing a meta-perspective on anti-oppressive practice.

Empowerment: as reflective practice

This draws on the work of Donald Schon (1991) and involves a rigorous approach to reflecting on practice, and reformulating goals and methods of working, as the action proceeds. Social work, among other human services professions, is viewed as requiring an approach to practice based on reflection-in-action, rather than the technical/rational approach typical of those professions, such as engineering and the law where the knowledge base is less uncertain and the technologies for carrying out the work are more established and clearcut.

Empowerment: as a ladder

Arnstein distinguishes different relationships between workers and community members, by references to a hierarchical image: a ladder from the most controlling or manipulative at the lowest rungs, through to the fully participative at the top rungs (Arnstein, 1969). If the concept of empowerment were to be transposed back through time to the late 1960s, then it is likely that Arnstein would have conceived this typology of citizen participation in terms of the degree of empowerment or disempowerment embodied in each position. Implicitly, the image of the ladder conveys a value judgement about higher positions being preferable.

Empowerment: consciousness-raising through a dialogic process

Freire's contribution (referred to in more detail in Chapter 4) is to provide a model whereby the consciousness-raising process can link the circumstances of the individual with those of the social context, thereby providing a route to empowerment in the different domains, focused on the individual in society.

A generic means of anti-oppressive practice

Phillipson portrays a hierarchy of anti-oppressive practice from specialist feminist practice, through the specific area of anti- sexist practice practice to the universal level of anti-oppressive practice. She locates empowerment at the top of this hierarchy, implying that it is the universal means to achieve liberation.

Framework for empowerment-in-practice

The framework in Figure 2.1 is proposed as a way in which social work theory and practice can advance, at the confluence of empowerment, at whatever level, and critically reflective practice. As suggested above, this framework has the merit of containing elements of the thinking of Freire, Schon and Phillipson, without being dogmatically prescriptive. Yet it provides two axes in terms of which it is argued clarity needs to be reached: first, the domain or level of empowerment and second, the extent to which practice is reflective. Without reflective practice, the contextual constraints referred to earlier in this chapter are likely to make empowerment a rather rhetorical term, without substance in practice. In this book, the term 'empowerment-in-practice' is used to indicate the synergy between reflective practice and empowerment.

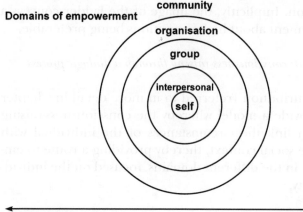

Domains of empowerment

community
organisation
group
interpersonal
self

Technical/rationality   Reflection-in-Action
Disempowering   Empowering
              Extent of reflectiveness-in-practice

Figure 2.1 *Framework for empowerment-in-practice*

This framework, for the horizontal dimension of which I
have drawn heavily on Schon's work (1991), highlights the
need to clarify the two key components of empowering activity: the level at which it takes place and the extent to which
the worker acts reflectively. The synergy between these two
components creates empowerment-in-practice.

Domains of empowerment

The use of the term 'domain' provides a way out of the perpetuation of the hierarchical language of levels. Similarly, the
use of concentric circles indicating the different levels for empowering activity, indicates that the outer circles of activity
include those inside them and avoids implying that one level
is higher than another.

Extent of reflectiveness in practice

On the horizontal dimension, the distinctive features of the
human services need recognition, and the particular signific-

ance of social work emerges as a point of conjuncture and theorising and practice development concerning empowerment-in-practice – though it does not always overlap – for disciplines, professions and organisations in the human services. Some of the major aspects of the divergence between technical/rationality and reflection-in-action, identified by Schon, can be elaborated on and represented schematically as in Figure 2.2.

Technical /rationality	Reflection-in-action
(*Disempowering*)	(*Empowering*)
Personal/professional:	
Fragmented	Holistic
Segregated	Integrated
Trained	Lifelong learner
Acquiescent/oppressed	Assertive/empowered
Work:	
Technical/habit	Reflective/practice
Approaches:	
Convergent	Divergent
Solution focused	Problematic focused
Problem solving	Problem describing
Perspective:	
Positivist	Postmodern
Evaluation:	
Experimental	Experiment-in- practice
(hypothesis testing) method	
Observer/scientist	Experient/co-producer

Figure 2.2 *Aspects of disempowering and empowering practice*

The use of the domains axis of the framework as the structure for the next five chapters should not be taken as an endorsement of a simple mechanistic application of the sequence from self-empowerment through to community empowerment. We shall indicate in succeeding chapters the major reasons why this is not the case and also point out some key issues which are likely to need addressing in the process of implementation. In this area, as in so much of social work, meaningful practice development is a struggle for authenticity, in a context where very little can be taken for granted as unproblematic. A feature of the framework, and a practical limitation imposed by the length of this book, is that many aspects of the framework remain unexplored. However, the material in the first edition of this book has been reworked so as to give indications as to how to develop an empowering practice. This is consistent with implementing empowerment-in-practice, thereby rejecting the idea of a template which can simply be placed over a given situation to produce a 'right answer'.

3
Self-Empowerment

Introduction

It could be argued that before empowering other people, workers need to become empowered themselves. Whether or not empowerment-in-practice begins with the self, there is certainly a place for considering one's own thoughts, feelings and situation in any work with other people. Importantly though, this does not imply a psychologised, rather than a social, vision of empowerment-in-practice. Adequately theorised, empowerment-in-practice must be realised in all domains self, individual, group, organisation and community. Also, self-empowerment, and hence this chapter, applies equally to workers and service users. So, the purpose of this chapter is not to suggest that self-empowerment is the key to all other aspects, but to argue that the person who feels and is empowered, is more likely to have the motivation and capacity to empower other people, and to be empowered by them. Also, it is important to emphasise that a re-vision of empowerment is required, which recognises its impact on the self, before engaging with service users and other people's movement towards their own self-realisation. This chapter considers how to achieve this goal. It involves the development of areas of expertise, with the purpose of self-realisation and personal fulfilment, but not at the expense of other people. A balance should be struck between one person's empowerment and another person's disempowerment. If empowerment involves an equality-based practice, then it is inadmissible to engage in self-empowerment at another person's expense. In other words, 'good' self-empowerment should, by definition, empower other people.

This chapter owes much to Phillipson (1992), whose CCETSW publication on gender, oppression and learning has proved an invaluable stimulus and source of ideas.

Approaches to self-empowerment

Self-empowerment is one of the most neglected aspects of empowerment theory and practice. In one sense, this is not surprising, since in the social work literature one of the most marginalised aspects is probably the personal and professional development of the social worker. In another sense, it demonstrates a failure to take on board the implications of the paradigm of empowerment. To this end, the framework outlined in Chapter 2 offers an holistic approach, which focuses attention on oneself.

Almost every approach to self-help, self-instruction, self-development and self-education has an empowering dimension. This chapter will not attempt to survey such a vast field. Instead, the focus will be upon some illustrations which have particular relevance to social work and empowerment-in-practice.

Using self-empowerment as the basis for collectively challenging oppression

Alan Stanton notes that the empowerment of workers is a prerequisite, before they go on to empower other people (Stanton, 1990, p. 122). His argument is justified by research into social services agencies, such as law and advice centres and Women's Aid refuges, which are attempting to manage themselves.

Stanton's analysis is presented in a provocative and stimulating account, which emphasises the need for self-empowerment of workers to challenge a deferential and oppressive agency culture and develop a democratic way of working towards the goal of self-empowerment and empowerment of service users. Broadening the analysis from agency-based to any workers, it seems likely that workers engaged in self-empowerment will need to do so from

- a commonly agreed value base (Stanton, 1990, p. 124)
- an analysis of unequal or oppressive features of the situation of individuals
- clear strategies for addressing areas of inequality and oppression
- a repertoire of relevant areas of expertise to be drawn on
- access to learning resources to enable other essential expertises to be developed
- an open style of working together (Stanton, 1990, p. 128)
- a close fit between the empowerment of the workers as service providers and the empowerment of the service users (Stanton, 1990, p. 129).

Reflective practice

At the heart of empowerment-in-practice are two sets of ideas referred to in Chapter 2: the process of conscientisation set out by Freire (1986) and the activities associated with reflection-in-practice, described by Schon (1991). Self-empowerment involves one aspect of reflective practice. In some senses, the process of experiment in practice as described by Schon and investigation and critical reflection proposed by Freire, are both attempts to capture in words what adult educators in general, and social work educators in particular, have been grappling with for years: how to facilitate learning in an empowering way. The focus on self-empowerment in this chapter means that these ideas concentrate on oneself.

The broader field of reflective practice and self-empowerment

The concept of reflective practice can be applied not only in the human services but also in the disciplines of the social science and humanities which provide the knowledge base underpinning their practice. Reflective practice increasingly provides a rationale for both research in these disciplines and the education and training of practitioners in, for example, social work.

Likewise, the scope of self-empowerment is much broader than just social work. Health and social services apart, contemporary self-empowerment includes such aspects as agricultural self-sufficiency, alternative communities and communes and worker participation in industry (Stokes, 1981, pp. 18–19).

The process of self-empowerment may be divided into continously repeated, and to some extent inseparable, overlapping stages: assessment and planning, action and reflection.

Assessment and planning

Clarifying the starting point for self-empowerment

It is worth attempting to frame the situation from which self-empowerment starts as though it was like many other learning situations. This should generate a number of key questions, which may help to clarify the potential strengths and weaknesses of the situation. A person's personal profile should include details of the situation in which learning takes place. What barriers exist? What learning opportunities are there? What supports for the learning process exist? What level of resources – access to libraries, accessibility to learning opportunities and other learners and colleagues – are there? How relevant are the resources of time to learn and somewhere to learn, at this stage in the process? What sorts of skills and previous learning and experiences can be brought to bear on the current situation?

Clarifying areas for self-development

One way forward with the planning is to continue with the educational model and develop a strategy based on the notion of adult learning. This may involve nothing more than sorting out a list of areas relevant to self-development. At the other extreme, it may lead to registering on a formal programme dealing with an aspect of personal and/or professional development. Or, it may involve informal, independent study on some topic considered to be relevant. The advantages of this exercise of clarification, though, are in terms of the development of knowledge about one's preferred personal learning styles and learning needs, as well as in the possible increase in self-confidence which may result.

Learning styles and profiles

People learn in different ways. Some adult learning programmes include materials enabling people to find out more about their preferred learning styles and to develop learning profiles, charting particular areas of personal preference and interest. Some profiles include self-assessment schedules, to enable inventories of personal skills to be developed. One such programme, the Health and Social Services Management Programme, for managers in health and social care, is published by the Open University and includes a workbook entitled 'Learning to Learn' in its first module 'Personal and Team Effectiveness' (Salaman, Adams and O'Sullivan, 1994). This material is designed for flexible use by an individual, who may use it for college, work or home-based study.

Formulating a self-empowerment plan

The next stage is to prepare a plan. The plan should include reference to the goals, the methods of attaining them, the areas of existing expertise on which the individual will draw, the new areas of expertise which will be needed, when and how these will be gained, what resources – including time, money and people – may be drawn on, and over what time period the plan will be carried out.

Action

Action involves doing and, at least in theory, is incompatible with reflection. But as Schon admits, practitioners often think about what they are doing while they are doing it (Schon, 1991, p. 275). The important thing is not to take this doing for granted, but to consider very carefully how to make the best use of it, with the aim of self-empowerment. The following are some pointers to action.

Carrying out the self-empowerment plan

Implementing the plan typically will involve a good deal of effort, spent on aspects such as negotiating space to do the work and organising time to complete various tasks. Access to resources, including learning materials where appropriate, will need to be found. There will be a need to manage time and effort carefully, so as not to lose these scarce resources. One's commitment to the task is vulnerable and should be nurtured in a self-interested way.

Addressing barriers to self-empowerment

Not only the practice, but also the conceptual basis – the language and grammar – of self-empowerment are currently in the process of development, implying that measures for self-empowerment by individuals will involve a struggle. Sometimes the struggle will be for resources, at other times it will be against one's own attitudes or the barriers may exist at the level of the attitudes of other people, the group, the institution or the social structure. For example, a disabled person who wishes to join an ongoing adult education programme in management may find it permeated with disablist assumptions at the structural, group, interpersonal and individual levels. If non-disabled people outnumber disabled people in the programme, if the tutor does not practise disability awareness, there is even more need for the individual to be prepared and able to address the issues. This same consciousness-raising process needs to extend to one's own thoughts and feelings.

There is a need for many practitioners to engage the assistance of a consultant, supervisor or mentor, to examine, for example, how to keep self-aware of areas of oppression and aspects where one's thoughts and feelings are not in touch with each other. Knowing-and-feeling is an holistic act central to empowerment-in-practice. This is easy to skate over, but very difficult to realise in practice. People need resources for consultation consistent with their individual circumstances. The fact that this implies that women, black people and disabled people are paired in consultant–consultee relationships where required by the worker, should be regarded as an aspect of the worker's rights, and not diagnosed as a sign of personal weakness or difficulty.

Addressing aspects of inequality

Such inequalities as exist in one's situation may not always be obvious. For example, discrimination may lead to disabled people, or women, being excluded from certain activities by other people in group settings, simply by the way non-disabled people and men are favoured by a facilitator in a discussion group. Research points to the tendency for men in group learning situations to receive more than their fair share of attention, and to behave more assertively than women. It is important for women to prepare themselves to challenge such imbalances (Phillipson, 1992, pp. 44–5). The responsibility should not be put on women to attend to the gendering of learning situations. But it is a prerequisite that women develop techniques of self-empowerment, which will enable them to tackle such issues. Key skills in this regard include gender awareness and assertiveness, including the challenging of routines and language which are disempowering.

Assertiveness, self-actualisation and personal growth

The domain of self-empowerment draws in part on insights from psychology and social psychology concerning self-development to maximise personal growth and human potential. It is based on the assumption that people themselves can make a decisive contribution to the self-set goal of realising their own potential and making the most of relationships with other people. An example is the growing field of assertiveness training, which people may undertake in their own time, or which may form part of an inservice training programme. The *Dictionary of Social Work* defines assertiveness as 'behaviours and thoughts that have at their root a concern to establish interests or rights either of oneself or of others' (Thomas and Pierson, 1995, p. 27). Some literature on self-help and assertion in the early 1980s may be criticised for its emphasis on the aggressive, even *macho* image it espoused (Lindenfield, 1986). Later publications focus more on self-realisation and techniques which avoid confrontation and enable the individual to acquire expertise in facilitating other people in developing their own potential. The assertive person enables others to achieve self-realisation.

Reflection

Reflection – thinking about the action – is a repeated, if discontinuous process. It involves taking snapshots, describing and interpreting to oneself or others, whilst in the midst of practice (Schon, 1991, pp. 276–8).

Reflexivity and self-empowerment

Reflexivity involves those aspects of experience and reflection which impact on oneself. Reflexivity is the dynamic process of using one's responses to practice to inform critical reflection on it. At the same time, self-empowerment is the reflexive dimension of empowerment. It is easier to say what it involves than what it is. It involves those areas of the self – knowledge, values and skills, thinking, feeling, sensitivity, self-awareness – which require development together with professional development. This does not mean that personal and professional development are separable, but that professional expertise tends to receive more attention than the personal aspects of development. This is unfortunate because, as the literature on occupational health and such topics as 'burn-out' and stress indicate, the worker as a whole person requires investment; it is short-sighted for employers to use staff without attention to the non-managerial supervision, consultation, support and development opportunities they require.

Example: Perspective transformation

A feature of very useful approaches is that they tend to be passed on from one person to another. Thus, the notion of perspective transformation which Phillipson illustrates below, is based on Freire's process of conscientisation (see Chapter 4) and has been used by Jack Mezirow (1983). Phillipson's comments are worth quoting at length:

> Mezirow's ideas spring from working with women in re-entry into learning programmes, in which they came to question and see afresh their previously held beliefs about the 'proper' roles of women. By a process of sharing and trying out different options and behaving, they came to new ways of seeing and acting, a process that Freire call 'conscientization'.

Mezirow details 10 stages involved in perspective transformation starting with a disorienting dilemma, moving on to self-examination, and through a 'critical assessment of personally internalised role assumptions and a sense of alienation from traditional role expectations' to trying new roles and behaving differently. While Mezirow's model was refined during working with women returners, the model is equally useful for working with men. Many men are discomforted by some of the traditional expectations of masculinity, and perspective transformation offers a route to unlearning, re-framing and change that men can work on together.

Two simplified examples illustrate some dilemmas which might be a starting point. One male student learnt of the research on the sexual division of labour in group discussions; acquiring this knowledge posed him with a dilemma concerning how much and when he should speak. Another had been told by both his female partner and by his daughter that he often did not listen yet he saw himself as a sympathetic and intelligent listener. This feedback from his family made him question his own sense of himself and his skills as a practitioner; he wasn't sure what kind of listening they were talking about. Discussing dilemmas such as these, unravelling the power relationships rooted in the institutionalised ideologies which we have absorbed (e.g. about talking and listening), then trying out different ways of behaving could pave the way for the more challenging dilemmas that social work practice reveals, for example, about child sexual abuse. (Phillipson, 1992, pp. 46–7)

This chapter has shown that self-empowerment is not the monopoly of the professional and that self-empowerment involves attempting to infuse anti-oppressive practices throughout the process of empowerment-in-action. It is at least a working hypothesis, if not an unambiguous conclusion, that a person who feels disempowered will find it more difficult than a person who feels empowered, to work with other people towards their own empowerment. But at the heart of self-empowerment involving the worker, colleagues and service users among others, is the need to transcend the simplistic mechanical notion of self-empowerment as the precursor of empowerment of other people. If empowerment is not to replicate and multiply the oppressiveness of the societal and professional contexts which it inhabits, then it needs to be employed with due attention to the mutuality of exchanges between people, in their respective sites of self-empowerment. Thus, although separated for the purposes of structuring this book, from the topic of empowering other individuals which now follows, the concepts inherent in this chapter cannot be disentangled from that and the succeeding chapters.

4

Empowering Individuals

Introduction

This chapter deals with the area of empowering individual
people. Until the 1980s, there was a dearth of research and
practice development drawing on psychological theories related to empowerment. Whilst it is true that empowerment
involves the key roles of social workers, its significance is that
potentially it represents an added dimension in all of them.
Much of the literature takes for granted that individual
people will not have to overcome difficulties in becoming involved in self-empowerment, empowering groups, networks
and community organisations. In fact, traditional social work
either ignores deliberately or by default the disempowerment
implicit in people's everyday circumstances. Workers tend to
expect the person to adjust to the normality of things as they
are, rather than to join in a reframing of them, perhaps as a
struggle against oppression. This chapter examines a number
of ways in which empowerment-in-practice provides an alternative to contributing to the adjustment of individuals to the
status quo, or more reprehensible still, simply controlling
them, thereby suppressing their wants and needs. In some
areas of practice, though, we must recognise that social workers are mainly acting as controllers of people. In such circumstances, it may be unrealistic to pretend that much, if
any, empowerment-in-practice can take place.

This chapter rebuts any implication that having empowered themselves, workers to empower can, and should,
proceed straightforwardly to empower other people. Whilst

there is a logical link between self-empowerment and empowering other individuals, this is an heuristic feature of the framework; that is, there is no necessarily causal connection between the two sets of activity. However, Freire's work is referred to below because it provides a now classic model for how consciousness- raising forges links between personal empowerment and the social dimension of people's circumstances.

Empowering work with individuals

Whilst some of the work social workers do takes place with and within groups, interaction between individuals forms a more basic, though different ingredient. Before groups can work effectively to empower people, individuals in them need to feel empowered. One of the key implications of the examples at the end of this chapter is that before groups can work effectively to empower people, individual members of them may need empowering. The worker needs to develop ways of working with individuals which empower them.

But not all interactions between the worker and the service user are likely to have an equal potential for empowering the person. One way of addressing this is to assess the empowering potential of different approaches to working with individuals. To start at a basic level, we could pose the question as to how the paradigm of empowerment can be applied in everyday practice. We test this by taking a standard text on working with individuals and trying to generate examples of empowering practice which relate to the various types of work.

Heron has categorised counselling intervention into two categories: authoritative and facilitative. Authoritative work – prescriptive, informative and confronting – involves the more overt exercise of control; facilitative work – cathartic, catalytic and supportive – is less overtly directive (Heron, 1990). Heron calls the first three authoritative because they are more hierarchical and involve the practitioner taking responsibility on behalf of the client. The facilitative interventions are less hierarchical and involve the practitioner enabling clients to become more autonomous and take responsibility for themselves. Heron's analysis is across different professional contexts, including medicine, nursing, social work, business management and counselling, teaching in secondary and higher education, policing and youth and community work. Its value, from the point of view of empowerment, is in distinguishing those social work activities which may be less amenable to empowerment (the first three) from those which lend themselves to empowerment more readily (the second three).

Heron argues that whilst the six categories are independent of each other, in that there is a sense in which each cannot be reduced to the form of any other, they overlap significantly in certain respects. For example, information giving may be confronting, prescription may be catalytic (Heron, 1990, p.7). For the sake of representativeness in this book on empowerment, a further category – advocacy – has been added to the facilitative group of activities.

Authoritative

These are not excluded from empowering work, but it has to be acknowledged that tensions need managing. For example, leading people to make decisions is not inconsistent with these activities, but it can hardly be described as mainstream empowerment. The question is whether the use of empowerment is of central relevance to these authoritative activities. The response to this is that whilst examples of each are hard to find, the situation of the service user or client is probably improved by the attempt to relate work done under each heading to empowerment. The challenge is how to engage with the service user in an empowering way, given the limitations imposed by the context and the role the worker is required to carry out.

1. *Prescriptive* This intervention seeks to direct the behaviour of the service user; this may involve the worker applying the law to control the service user. Paradoxically, the worker may be able to act so as to clarify the personal rights of the service user and thereby leave that person empowered to act and respond, whilst the social worker fulfils the directive role.

2. *Informative* This seeks to give knowledge, information and meaning to the client. In this situation, the worker can ensure that the service user can enter into dialogue about expectations of what use the information may be and how it could be empowering. Thus, in community care, for example, as has been noted (Smale, Tuson, Biehal and Marsh, 1993, p. 5), people may object to being made to feel powerless, by having to undergo the process of having their needs assessed and a care plan devised and implemented, managed by a professional, such as a social worker. It may be preferable to hand them information and resources to enable them to have direct access to their chosen services.

3. *Confronting* This seeks to raise the awareness of the service user about some limiting attitude or behaviour of which she or he is relatively unaware. The process of marital work with separating and divorcing couples, for example, may necessitate the use of techniques in which the worker exercises authority rather than empowering (Dingwall, 1988). However, it should still be possible to act as in prescriptive work to inform the person at the outset of personal rights, so as to hand over responsibility to respond, and perhaps dissent, from what is being presented. This is a very exposing and challenging role to expect the social worker to undertake. But it should be borne in mind that the person confronted is being challenged at least as much, and there is a correspondingly greater responsibility to empower the person. Barber quotes Fosterling (1985) as identifying further strategies for countering helplessness. These include using social

reinforcement, or praise, persuasion by means of modelling and group pressure, and confronting people with information incompatible with their existing negative attributional style (Barber, 1991, p. 40).

Facilitative

The following facilitative activities offer the worker more obviously empowering potential than authoritative roles. Various facilitative approaches – cognitive work, radical therapy, family therapy, brief therapy, transactional analysis, existential social work – would lay claim to working in an empowering way. Thompson gives the example of the use of counselling and other similar methods, to boost a disabled person's self-confidence, and advocacy to promote her or his status as a citizen. This contrasts with their starting situation:

> disenfranchised by marginalisation, isolation and dehumanisation – at a personal level through prejudice and misdirected pity; and at a cultural level through negative stereotypes and values; at a structural level through a society dominated by capitalist notions of 'survival of the fittest' and charity for those who are 'handicapped' from competing. (Thompson, 1993, p. 127)

4. *Cathartic*   This seeks to enable the service user to discharge painful emotions, including grief and anger, for example. It can be carried out so as to begin with the experience of the person and the process can be continued at the pace and in the direction the person indicates, so as to be consistent with meeting needs.

5. *Catalytic*   This seeks to enable the service user to engage in self-discovery, self-directed living, learning and problem solving. Again, the starting point of the process can be agreement with the person about how to proceed and in what direction, so as to maximise personal empowerment.

6. *Supportive* This seeks to affirm the worth and value of the personal qualities, attitudes and actions of the service user. The purpose of supportive work can be fulfilled, by building on the feelings and thoughts of the person and developing the work in an empowering way.

7. *Advocacy* This includes a range of activities from citizen advocacy to advocacy by the worker. There are several types of advocacy – individual: citizen, self, by carers, by profession-als and collective: for change affecting a category or group of people. Individual advocacy for or with people is vulnerable to the charge that it compromises their autonomy and inde-pendence as empowered persons.

One of the most apt illustration of collective self-advocacy is Survivors Speak Out, an organisation in the field of mental health. It was formed in Britain in 1986 'to promote awareness of the real possibility of recipient action and to improve per-sonal contact and the flow of information between individuals and groups' (Lawson, 1991, p. 73). Survivors' groups such as Survivors Speak Out include former patients such as people who have been in mental hospitals and have spread in recent years through many Western countries. Some have well-estab-lished networks of contact people, furthered in some cases by magazines or newsletters. In Survivors Speak Out, both 'sys-tems survivors' and 'allies' are working together in this organi-sation to develop self-advocacy (Survivors Speak Out, *Newsheet*, 1988). After the first national conference of users of psychia-tric services in September 1987, one user said 'This weekend has been more helpful to me through mutual support than many years of medication ever were.' Another who chose to attend rather than be admitted to a psychiatric hospital said: 'My consultant wanted to admit me. I chose to come here. I can only thank everyone because coming here has done me far more good than any mental hospital ever could' (*Survivors Speak Out Newsheet*, 1988).

Survivors' groups such as Survivors Speak Out become affiliated to a radical agenda for change in the policy and practice of mental health, but at the same time individuals may seek basic support and help from the group itself. We can see this paradox operating more clearly in the areas of women's therapy groups.

Process of empowering individuals

Having collated a number of examples of empowering work with individuals, we now examine a possible conceptual basis for the process of empowering the individual. This requires reference both to the psychological processes and to the structural context within which the interaction between the worker and the person is located. The work of Paulo Freire is a means of accomplishing this.

The basis for empowering individuals lies in research and practice regarding the surmounting of oppression. Psychological insights are essential to an understanding of the process of empowerment. The work of Paulo Freire (1986) provides a key reference point, building on his experience in South America. The entire thrust of Paulo Freire's work on consciousness-raising and empowerment was informed by his basic analysis that the individual's state of mind – the psychological dimension of the process of empowerment – was the priority to be tackled. Freire was concerned to engage in a process of consciousness-raising with poor people, to the point where they could overcome their economic, cultural, intellectual and emotional oppression and challenge their dependence and powerlessness. Freire's concept of consciousness-raising, to which he applied the term 'conscientization', means 'learning to perceive social, political, and economic contradictions, and to take action against the oppressive elements of reality' (Freire, 1986, p. 15).

Freire uses everyday terms in a special way to capture the essence of the process of overcoming oppression and empowering people. Thus, the heart of the process is dialogue between people, the encounter in which the united reflection and action of the dialoguers are addressed to the world which is to be transformed and humanized, this dialogue cannot be reduced to the act of one person's 'depositing' ideas in another, nor can it become a simple exchange of ideas to be 'consumed' by the participants in the discussion . . . Because dialogue is an encounter among men who name the world, it must not be a situation where some men name on behalf of others. It is an act of creation; it must not serve as a crafty instrument for the domination of one man by another. (Freire, 1986, pp. 61–2)

Dialogue, education and criticality go hand in hand: 'Only dialogue, which requires critical thinking, is also capable of generating critical thinking. Without dialogue there is no communication, and without communication there can be no true education.' Again, 'true dialogue cannot exist unless it involves critical thinking' (Freire, 1986, p. 64). In order to achieve dialogue, people require words.

But the word is more than just an instrument which makes dialogue possible; accordingly, we must seek its constituent elements. Within the word we find two dimensions, reflection and action, in such radical interaction that if one is sacrificed – even in part – the other immediately suffers. There is no true word that is not at the same time a praxis. Thus, to speak a true word is to transform the world. (Freire, 1986, p. 60)

Barriers to empowerment

Clearly, the barriers to empowerment may reflect those inequalities associated with ageism, racism, sexism, 'classism', disablism and other dimensions which contribute to people's oppression. Classism is often swept aside amid the flurry of activity around the prominent 'isms'. Michael Lerner (1979) wrote of the 'surplus powerlessness' of the working classes in developed countries. Lerner used this term to describe the psychological burden which oppressed people carry with them and which, if not challenged and modified, acts as a script for their future actions.

Empowering individual people draws extensively on psychological theories of empowerment, and particularly on the psychology of powerlessness. Examples of the significant developments, particularly in the USA, of psychological strategies – specifically cognitive and behavioural – aimed at empowering people by enabling them to feel in control, are provided by Baistow (Rappaport, 1984; Swift and Levin, 1987; Wallerstein, 1992; Zimmerman and Rappaport, 1988, referred to in Baistow, 1994). Interestingly, Baistow notes that such approaches may provide opportunities for professionals to enhance, rather than reduce, their regulatory control of service users' lives, through such approaches to user empowerment (Baistow, 1994, p. 39).

We can look in more detail at the psychology of individual empowerment through the work of Barber. Barber has identified two critical moments in the development of powerlessness, or the psychological state of helplessness: exposure to uncontrollability and the attitude that it would be useless to respond (Barber, 1991, p. 38). These theories resonate with research into not so much why people protest as, given the ongoing existence of many factors conducive to dissatisfaction, why people do not engage in collective protest more often (Adams, 1991, p. 9).

Barber (1991, pp. 32–3) refers to the application to people of Seligman's (1975) behavioural studies of dogs to illustrate the development of 'learned helplessness'. Learned helplessness is the state of mind which leaves people unable to see the point of engaging with a new task in view of a previous experience of failure, not necessarily in an identical situation, but sometimes in one with only some similarities. If unchallenged, 'the helpless individual will virtually give up and lie down' (Barber, 1991, p. 33). A further feature of learned helplessness which concerned Lerner was that even if 'helpless' people managed to achieve things, they tended to be unable to perceive that it was their efforts which led to positive outcomes, tending to explain them in terms of factors external to themselves. Lerner regarded this theory as helping to explain why some of the left-wing activists did not capitalise on their successes in the 1960s and 1970s (Lerner, 1979, p. 19, quoted in Barber, 1991, p. 34). Again, learned helplessness may have the negative effect of producing paralysing rather than motivating fear in people, similar to the apathy experienced in depression (Seligman, 1975).

Overcoming barriers: empowering individuals and transforming the world

The contribution of Freire lies in the extraordinary vision of positive strategies linking individual empowerment with social change. He envisages praxis as the continuing means by which people 'create history and become historical-social beings' (Freire, 1986, p. 73). This involves replacing domination, 'the fundamental theme of our epoch' with liberation. He views this as a humanising process involving the elimination of oppression, transcending those situations which reduce people to things (Freire, 1986, p. 75). The key to action links critical reflection with investigation. This is an educational process of deepening historical awareness of people's situation. As people become aware of the conditions of their existence, they acquire the ability to intervene and change it (Freire, 1986, pp. 80–1).

Freire is wary of attempts to reduce the complex process of educating and conscientisation:

> Manipulation, sloganizing, 'depositing', regimentation, and prescription cannot be components of revolutionary praxis, precisely because they are components of the praxis of domination. In order to dominate, the dominator has no choice but to deny true praxis to the people, deny them the right to say their own word and think their own thoughts. He cannot act dialogically; for him to do so would mean either that he had relinquished his power to dominate and joined the cause of the oppressed, or that

he had lost that power through miscalculation. . . . It is absolutely essential that the oppressed participate in the revolutionary process with an increased awareness of their role as Subjects of the transformation. If they are drawn into the process as ambiguous beings, partly themselves and partly the oppressors housed within them – and if they come to power still embodying that ambiguity imposed on them by the situation of oppression – it is my contention that they will merely *imagine* they have reached power. Their existential duality may even facilitate the rise of a sectarian climate leading to the installation of bureaucracies which undermine the revolution . . . They may aspire to revolution as a means of domination, rather than as a road to liberation. (Freire, 1986, pp. 97–8)

Empowerment which transcends the domain of individual work

Before moving to empowering groups, communities and organisations, it may help to develop a practice which empowers individuals. Barber views the goal of empowering individuals as enabling them to become more self-directive and assertive, and enabling them to develop optimism that engaging in collective work with others is likely to lead to constructive outcomes (Barber, 1991, p. 41). The following two examples are of strategies for empowering individuals, which cross the boundary into work with groups.

Baistow has correctly identified the weakness of attempting to deal with the psychologically-based approaches to empowerment separately from group and community-based empowerment, as though these levels either are best left mutually segregated. It is as though the empowered person and the empowered group and/or community fuse without the need for further work, or explanation. The following two examples anticipate the subject matter of later chapters and offer insights into two kinds of transition. In the first example, work takes place with individuals to enable them to take key roles in running groups for themselves, without professional leadership. The second example involves the process of individual consciousness-raising, linked with a structure which enables gender-based community groups to develop, through which women, once empowered, are able to challenge key oppressive features of a male-dominated society.

Example 1: Mind Your Self

In the following illustration, before a carefully structured, significant level of support was formulated for groups, they tended to collapse, either because members were demotivated at the outset because of their state of mind, or because they lacked the confidence, skills and/or resources to run the activities effectively.

Mind Your Self is a Leeds-based project founded in the late 1970s and originally sponsored by the Leeds Association for Mental Health. It consists of a network of groups, short-course and other associated activities in which non-professional empowermenters have a leading part, the support of a professional social worker and other workers playing a crucial role. The history of the project illustrates the nature of facilitation by the professional, who began to offer therapeutic support to groups of people with mental health problems in an attempt to counteract the tendency for their groups to be short-lived failures (Adams and Lindenfield, 1985, p. 19). The barriers encountered by group members to running their own groups are typical of the kinds of problems which may act as barriers to empowering individuals with mental health problems. Thompson identifies the medicalisation of mental health problems – which gives considerable power to medical professionals – and stereotypes of mentally ill people embodied in the medical model of mental illness, as two obstructions to the empowerment of people with mental health problems. He shows firstly how people diagnosed as mentally ill are defined, stigmatised and consequently disempowered. Secondly, he points out that the medical definition of mental illness separates the distress felt by the individual from its wider social context, thus reducing the assessment of the complex circumstances of the person being treated to simple pathology, rather than the underlying social, moral, political and economic factors receiving attention (Thompson, 1993, p. 143). The worker identified with members of groups the following problems they experienced: 'low self-esteem, lack of assertiveness, poor communication skills, lack of spontaneity, lack of physical energy, inability to trust, inability to take risks and no goals or sense of direction' (Adams and Lindenfield, 1985, p. 20). They produced a list of the qualities groups need in order to be effective: even participation, effective leadership, clear goals, good communication, ability to act and flexibility (Adams and Lindenfield, 1985, p. 21). 'As a result of this, we made a bargain. If they agreed to continue meeting weekly on their own, every third week I would work with them on these problems as a therapist. As a result, the group began to flourish. Several very good leaders emerged and began to take responsibility. A new partnership was born in this way, between myself and the group' (Adams and Lindenfield, 1985, p. 21).

In Mind Your Self, it appears that the general lack of problems of members becoming violent or refusing to leave a group, reflects a shared philosophy in groups of a good deal of individual freedom on the one hand and a measure of collective responsibility for behaviour on the other. However, it has been noted in Mind Your Self that the need for members involved in leading groups to have some kind of consultancy or supervision from outside the groups is as important for non-professionals as it is for professionals.

Perhaps a pay-off of this form of facilitation is the growth in confidence of group members. Members of Mind Your Self have begun to consider organising short courses on such topics as 'Diet', 'Getting Out of a Rut' and 'Middle Age'. The innovative features of Mind Your Self exemplify the relative willingness of people in the voluntary sector to take risks, in contrast with many of their counterparts in statutory social work agencies.

Whilst the strength of this form of facilitation clearly lies in the availability of professional leadership, there is a risk that the social worker will perpetuate this, rather than withdrawing. The problem is how to pace the withdrawal so that individuals can feel competent and not experience disablement or the collapse of the activity.

Commentary

One key feature of this example is the likelihood that individual empowerment-in-practice will necessitate the professional facilitating other individuals developing skills as the route to their empowerment. The stages of this work, exemplified in Mind Your Self, were as follows:

- The worker becomes aware of a need for action.
- The worker shares this awareness with other members of the group.
- The worker and other members identify barriers to individuals participating as fully as they wish, and taking on running the group themselves.
- The worker and other members negotiate, and agree on, a strategy for addressing the need; this involves overcoming the barriers to empowerment of group members.
- The worker and other members work on skills development of group members.
- Once other members feel they can do the work themselves, the worker withdraws to a servicing role.

Example 2: Nijeri Kori

The fact that Britain is in part heir to a tradition of facilitation of self-help projects inherited from the Third World, invites illustration of a well-established scheme called Nijeri Kori, endeavouring to bring about the establishment of a network of consciousness-raising groups in Bangladesh as a means of empowering individual women living in an oppressive society. Nijeri Kori means literally 'we do it ourselves', and was started in the late 1970s by a couple of Bangladeshi people concerned to find a more productive approach to development than traditional strategies involving agriculture, co-operatives and health care and in which the political dimension was often lacking. Nijeri Kori now has about 120 staff, based in Dacca, Bangladesh, works in four or five of the poorest parts of the country, and concentrates on consciousness-raising and organising, through demystifying the powerlessness many people feel and giving them back some strength in collective action. Priority is also given to working with women.

Workers are drawn from the area, trained and sent back to live alongside the landless, poorest people. Over a period of working alongside people, they encourage informal discussion in a group, perhaps using a local event, a tragedy, as a means of bringing people together in mutual solidarity. Subsequently, groups are encouraged to meet for a couple of hours about once a week with the workers and chat about their children, the problems of not having enough money, clothes or land, and problems of relationship with their husbands. They tend not to call them meetings, but 'sitting together'. Because in that society women traditionally do not speak in mixed groups, women meet separately from men, until they have become confident enough to meet with the men. Later the groups meet without the worker and form a local committee, represented equally by members of women's group and men's groups.

The principle involves a lengthy process of talking and thinking and thereby raising the confidence of individual women in particular to speak out about their situation.

Nijeri Kori is supported partly by War on Want and the following extract is from an account given to the writer for this book by Helen Allison from that organisation. The process of gradually accumulating confidence among women in male-

dominated settings is reminiscent of situations in Britain
where groups are discriminated against and oppressed. However, the impact of this group on that situation over a period
of time emerges in the account:

> it's quite spectacular to see. In one area we went to we sat in this
> little bedroom. All the women were there and then as soon as the
> meeting started and we were introduced all the women left and
> all the men moved in and sat on the bed. So we said, 'Where are
> the women? We want to talk to the women.' So the message went
> out that we wanted to see the women. Four women came back in
> and they sat on the bed. So the men moved over to our side and
> then gradually over a period of half an hour or an hour more
> women came in until the room was crowded. And we sat there for
> about two hours talking to them and the men stayed quiet for that
> whole period and listened to the women, partly because we were
> there undoubtedly. But they didn't interrupt, they didn't contra-
> dict. Even though initially the women were very shy and hid their
> faces and giggled and looked embarrassed, they got over that and
> talked very straightforwardly about simple things like their kids
> and their money, but also about more complicated things like how
> they were involved in Nijeri Kori and what the group meant to
> them, what they see as the possibilities for change and what they
> would like to see for their kids in the future . . . The only way of
> bringing about significant change is where people can organise
> and demand it and it may take a long time but I think in the long
> run it's more significant than just changing political parties . . .
> The idea is that once people get more conscious and get more
> confident and begin to organise locally, that they can then decide
> for themselves where they want to go: they may decide to join a
> political party, they may decide to take local action, to make pro-
> tests against local injustice. There have been cases where people
> have actually marched on the local government office and de-
> manded certain things. They've also taken up specific cases, like
> women have protested about wife-beating, which is quite unheard
> of. If one member of a group has been beaten either by her hus-
> band or by her brother-in-law, the women protesting about this
> would go to the man and try to shame him in public. Meanwhile,
> if he was involved in Nijeri Kori then the men's group would also

be trying to tackle that issue and discussing it. (Interview with Helen Allison, War on Want, 1987)

Commentary

The following stages in the action can be identified:

- analysis by the sponsoring organisation, before any action
- identifying structural features of the oppressive society, including barriers to empowerment of women such as sexism and depriving women of a means of meeting, sharing their experiences and developing strategies for tackling their oppression
- developing strategy, to enable individuals to have space, to build individuals' confidence through sharing experiences, to provide a forum for individuals to exchange and develop collective strategies for action to challenge their oppression, to enable individuals and the group to exercise power on the basis of a pool of shared experience to which members can repeatedly refer back
- proselytising to other individuals
- moving beyond material goals to further aims
- engaging in collective dialogue with men/oppressors (hitherto forbidden by cultural tradition and practice) through structure of men's groups facilitated by sponsoring organisation.

Both of these examples deal with situations where there is a transition from the individual domain to the domain of groupwork. However, key questions need answering about the relevance of two particular situations to the generality of conditions in which this work may be undertaken. Baistow (1994, p. 36) observes that the task of how to conflate the personal and the political, delineated as necessary, for example, by Mullender and Ward (1991) and by Stevenson and Parsloe by 'helping people to think through a situation that troubles them and in doing so to link the external world

in which they live with the internal world of their feelings'
(Stevenson and Parsloe, 1993), is left unexplained. In an attempt further to address this difficult area, the next two chapters view this issue from the standpoint of the generality of
experiences of group-based empowerment-in-practice.

5
Empowering Groups: Mapping the Territory

Introduction

Not all groups are empowering. The question is what it is about groups which makes possible the empowerment of their members. We shall first map the different kinds of groups, with this aspect of groupwork particularly in mind. Then this chapter and the next consider how empowering work with groups is most likely to be effective.

Realism about what groupwork can achieve

Groupwork is characterised by adherents to particular frameworks, approaches and methods, each of whom tend to assert the superiority, and sometimes the exclusive benefits, accruing from their favoured way of working. In social work, a small number of terms have come to be attached more than others to empowerment. The general rationale for different approaches to groupwork is that it provides support for the individual, reduces the risk of isolation, offers a context in which personal skills can be developed and practised and a means by which an individual whose consciousness has been raised, can work towards fulfilling heightened personal expectations. Mullender and Ward assert that 'groupwork can be immensely powerful if it is affiliated to a purpose which explicitly rejects the "splintering" of the public and private, of person and society' (1991, p. 12). Yet, as Baistow observes, the proposal of groupwork as an empowering strategy to counter oppression is based on a view 'of the "problem" as being implicitly amenable to psychological solutions. In this case the proposed solution is groupwork, in another, counselling' (Baistow, 1994, p. 36). One limitation on self-help or user-led groups arises from the potential conflict between the anti-oppressive principles Mullender and Ward (1991) claim as their basis and oppressive activities in which group members might engage. Should the professional facilitator intervene, thereby disempowering other members? (Page, 1992, p. 92)

Page sees the tangible achievements of Mullender and Ward's approach as likely to be extremely modest, and greater for the professional facilitators and educators than for other group members, unless the diverse pespectives of group members can be translated into more unified and realisable demands (Page, 1992, p. 92), *via* a coherent overarching strategy addressing the goal of collective consciousness-raising (Page, 1992, p. 90). Empowered groups may give their members a positive experience, but probably will not tackle wider problems, arising from poverty, joblessness, poor housing, inadequate health and social care services, and so on.

Features of empowering groups

Rather than attempt to encompass the entire range of groupwork, this chapter considers self-help and user-led groups. There is a lack of consensus in contemporary definitions of these. Some commentators, of course, talk as though self-help is purely associated with the efforts of individuals, whereas it often involves mutual aid. There is an ideological issue also, since to some people self-help is associated with the politics of the Right, so they tend to avoid the term, whereas radical activity also goes under its banner. At any rate, from the viewpoint of empowerment, the distinction is academic, although it should be noted that user-led groups are a particular category of self-help involving service users, whilst not all self-help groups are led by service users.

Self-help groups

Katz and Bender's definition of self-help as group activity is a good starting point. They say that self-help groups are:

> voluntary small group structures for mutual aid in the accomplishment of a specific purpose. They are usually formed by peers who have come together for mutual assistance in satisfying a common need, overcoming a common handicap or life-disrupting problem, and bringing about a desired social and/or personal change. (Katz and Bender, 1976, p. 9)

User-led groups

Mullender and Ward provide a conceptualisation of user-led groupwork, which they term work with self-directed groups. The model of self-directed groupwork they set out in their book grows out of the experience of workers and service users across the human services and is intended to apply in a range of professions, disciplines, settings and user groups (Mullender and Ward, 1991). Self-directed groupwork corresponds to the process of self-help described towards the end of this chapter. It focuses primarily on consciousness-raising and empowerment of group members. This involves the two major activities of analysis and action. Group members, in this case users, are supported in the early stages, the workers building the group with users as partners. This is to enable users to 'set the norms for the group, define and analyse the problems and set the goals' (Mullender and Ward, 1991, p. 18). Subsequently, users may move repeatedly through the sequence of clarifying problems and goals and taking action, as they take charge of the process with growing confidence. Finally, the users take over the group to the extent that the workers move into the background and may leave altogether.

Relationship between self-help and user-led groups

One of the features of the field of self-help and user-led groups is the great variety of practice. Some groups adopt a therapeutic mode, others are based on consciousness-raising. Some are led, or facilitated, by a professional worker, such as a social worker. Others, like self-directed groups, have designed into their framework a process whereby the worker starts by playing a key role as facilitator and progressively moves to a marginal, or even a non-participant, position. This corresponds to the three basic types of relationship between

Characteristic category of	Resourcing by organisation	Leadership by professional	Support by professional	Example of how profess- ional relates to self-help
INTEGRAL	Much or all	Direct	Regular	Innovates and makes activity available as part of service
FACILITATED	Some	Indirect	Intermittent	Stimulates activity
AUTONO- MOUS	None	None	None	Refers people to and imports learning

Figure 5.1 *Relationship between social work and self-help or user-led activity*

professionals and service users outlined below, depending on whether such groups are integral to, facilitated by, or autonomous from, the professionals.

Relationship between social worker and self-help/user-led groups

Figure 5.1 shows how three types of relationship between social work and self-help or user-led activity may be distinguished from each other, in terms of the degree of resourcing, leadership and support which comes from the professional organisation (which we are assuming here is normally a social work organisation) and the nature of the relationship between the professional and the self-help/user-led activity.

Using the analogy of driving, in the integral situation the worker is in the driving seat, in the facilitated situation the worker accompanies the hiring self-helper who takes the wheel, whilst in the autonomous situation the self-helper/service user owns the car and drives it independently of professional help.

Integral self-help

It will be evident from Figure 5.1 that this is the most paradoxical type of relationship, since self-help activities apparently are rooted in the social work agency and yet apparently exemplify the purposes and goals of self-help. This relationship involves activity promoted, supported and directly led by professionals in a social work organisation which largely or wholly sponsors the self-help. Gartner and Riessman (1977, p. 71) comment that the major health organisations are now sponsoring self-help clubs (for example, the American Cancer Society supports the laryngectomy, mastectomy and ostomy groups, and at a convention the American Heart Association recommended that its state affiliates encourage and promote the establishment of stroke clubs).

At first sight it looks as though integral self-help is a simple contradiction in terms. Integral self-help is difficult to reconcile with the simple statement that self-help necessarily is independent of all outside funding. What is more crucial, perhaps, is the need to clarify the relationship between self-helpers and professionals. Many are prepared to admit that professional guidance may play a legitimate part in self-help activity, though the structure and mode of operation must be under members' control. 'This definition thus rules out agency-sponsored and professionally led therapy groups as well as proprietary groups such as Weight-Watchers and Parents Anonymous, which . . . may utilise professionals among their ways of helping their members, when this seems indicated' (Levy, 1976, p. 306).

Examples of integral self-help include settings such as the independence unit in the social work facility, often using the work 'self-help' in its title, in which residents or service users involved in day-care are responsible for programming their own activities. They also include self-help groups organised and resourced entirely within a social work agency, but nevertheless run on self-help lines.

Facilitated self-help

This type of relationship occurs where social workers take enabling action to bring people together or create a climate for activity in some other way. It involves activity in which professionals provide some support and a degree of indirect leadership. Examples of such work come especially from areas of social work such as mental health, where a degree of professional knowledge, skill or resources at the preparatory or early stages of self-help can make the crucial difference between the survival or non-survival of an activity. It has thus been observed that people experiencing depression often find it hard to take the plunge and initiate a self-help group without some professional input in the form of knowledge, skills and resources (Lindenfield and Adams, 1984).

Autonomous self-help

Some self-help can be distinguished from other forms of helping in that people help themselves without recourse to professional social workers. That is, in the process of self-help they are not treated, given therapy, counselled or otherwise put into the situation of clients of social workers. This form of self-help is initiated, organised, resourced and run entirely independently of professionals. Clearly, the distance between the social worker and self-help can be seen most clearly in this type of independent relationship. Yet, in some senses, this sharpens the need for some articulation of that relationship itself. Again, as in the case of integral self-help, it seems at first glance as though this category of self-help has nothing to do with social work practice. But quite commonly, because of their subject matter, the issues they raise, as well as how their connections with social work are made, autonomous self-help activities deserve particular attention.

Autonomous self-help includes 'anonymous groups', survivors' groups, groups resisting stigma such as those in the disability movement, and consciousness-raising groups.

Some common features of self-help and user-led groups

In the medical context, Michael Moeller (1983, p. 69) suggests that self-help groups have six characteristics:

- All members are equal in status.
- Each makes decisions for herself or himself.
- The group is responsible for its own decisions.
- Each member joins because of her or his own problems.
- Group proceedings are confidential.
- Participation is free.

Knight and Hayes (1981, ch. 2) identify at least seven characteristics of self-help which apply particularly in the group setting: voluntary activity, members having shared problems, meetings for mutual benefit, sharing of the roles of helper and helped, constructive action towards shared goals, groups run by members and groups existing without outside funding. Pancoast's definition locates self-help as a kind of counterpoint, running alongside, and complementary with, formally provided services (Pancoast *et al.*, 1983, p. 19).

In a literature review, a very useful list of self-help characteristics has been identified: members sharing a common experience; mutual help and support; the helping of peers by those normally on the receiving end of help themselves; differential association by which people who wish to change decide to join groups in which existing members reinforce desired behaviour; collective willpower and belief in the group's values emphasising the fact that change is within members' capacities; information about which experiences and changes are likely to be encountered by a member of a group; and finally the use of activities as a constructive occurrence which members share in pursuing planned goals (Killilea, 1976, pp. 67–73).

A difficulty with Killilea's description is that it implies that activities focus on reinforcing desired behaviour and change for individual participants. Clearly, self-help occurs at different levels and focuses on other aspects besides people's problems. A complication in the context of empowerment is the fact that whilst social work and self-help are complementary in some respects, in others, self-help may function as an alternative to, or is actually in conflict with professional values.

Functions of self-help and user-led groups

Among self-help and user-led health groups we can distinguish those providing direct services from those concerned with ancillary activities such as research, education or campaigning activities. The latter are more likely to be older established and more secure, while the former are more loosely organised, informal and with small or non-existent operating budgets (Tracy and Gussow, 1976, p. 382).

Five kinds of self-help activity may be identified: therapeutic, social, educational, community action and research.

Therapeutic

The range of therapeutic activities is very wide and covers an equally wide variety of medical, remedial and social work areas. The emphasis is on facilities and treatments which either complement existing ones or act as alternatives.

Social

The generation of social activities is an unsurprising feature of those groups and organisations where people meet regularly. The provision of refreshments and outings often counterpoints the primary declared purposes of groups and organisations.

Educational

Usually, educational activities are directed at external individuals or agencies with the aim of raising their level of knowledge and awareness in the field covered by a particular group or organisation. Professionals may be a target, but participants may also want to inform each other and members of the general public. Courses, workshops and conferences may be organised in the more ambitious programmes.

Community action

Some self-help movements have the capacity to innovate and express activist sentiments at the community level. Working in Chicago before the Second World War, Saul Alinsky produced an approach to community action, exemplified by the Industrial Areas Foundation (Vattano, 1972, p. 12). Further, in Chicago in 1967 a gang of black youths called the Mighty Blackstone Rangers developed a degree of control over community disorder which reportedly ensured that their district of Woodlawns had no trouble. Other gangs in Negro districts in other parts of the US pursued a similar policy. In Nathan Caplan's study of riots in Detroit, he suggests that the interest the rioter and the anti-rioter both have in civil disorder brings them closer to each other than either is to the non-rioter (Dumont, 1971, pp. 152–3). In the 1970s, the author was involved in a community-based club, working with children and young people labelled as 'problems' by education and juvenile justice agencies, in West Yorkshire. One of the features of this work involved the children and young people working with adult project workers, a local community group and local volunteers to design and build an adventure playground on some waste ground. As was noted at the time, the emphasis on participation and on self-help within the club, like the shift towards community projects, was 'consistent with a move towards a "rights" approach and away from a "needs" approach' (Adams, 1981, p. 241). These examples highlight a feature of self-help – namely, that it tends to lie close to the way people involved in a given situation experience the problems and issues with which they are grappling.

Research

Some of the more established self-help organisations may, as indicated by Tracy and Gussow above, reach a point where public funds are allocated to research that they direct or co-ordinate. This research may have the aim of benefiting individuals suffering from a particular condition, or may serve the function of promoting pressure-group activity or a community action campaign.

Scope of self-help and user-led groups

The vast field of self-help and user-led groups is constantly changing. The everchanging character of groups makes it difficult to pin down their essential characteristics. Groups are coming into existence and disappearing all the time. In fact, Levy has noted that they change so quickly that a static directory of them is not much use (Levy, 1982, p. 1267). Yet there is a continuity in views of the scope of self-help, which stands independent of the vulnerability or short life of particular groups. Self-help groups range from problem-focusing through self-development to consciousness-raising.

Problem-focusing

Problem-focusing activities range from people's efforts to help themselves and each other with health problems such as eating disorders or substance abuse, to mental health problems such as depression and phobias and social problems such as loneliness. They include anonymous groups, relatives' and carers' groups, therapy groups and groups for people experiencing stigma. The growth of groups like Sexual Compulsives Anonymous, Excessives Anonymous, Sex Anonymous (in New York), Sex and Love Addicts Anonymous (in San Francis, Los Angeles and Boston) (Altman, 1986, p. 159), illustrate a growing movement towards self-help with what are perceived as sexual problems.

Anonymous groups   There is an ever-expanding list of groups modelling themselves on Alcoholics Anonymous (AA), the largest, most well known and probably the oldest of them all. They include Cancer Anonymous, Checks Anonymous, Convicts Anonymous, Crooks Anonymous, Delinquents Anonymous, Disturbed Children Anonymous, Divorcees Anonymous, Dropouts Anonymous, Fatties Anonymous, Gamblers Anonymous, Migraines Anonymous, Mothers Anonymous, Narcotics Anonymous, Neurotics Anonymous,

Parents Anonymous, Parents of Youth in Trouble Anonymous, Recidivists Anonymous, Relatives Anonymous, Retirees Anonymous, Rich Kids Anonymous, Schizophrenics Anonymous, Sexual Child Abusers Anonymous, Skin Anonymous, Smokers Anonymous, Stutterers Anonymous, Suicide Anonymous and Youth Anonymous (Gartner and Riessman, 1977, p. 25).

Well-established groups such as AA tend to have clearly specified principles covering their meetings and rules for members. AA displays in a form relatively unchanged since its founding in 1935, a number of principles, many of which are found also in other anonymous groups, including 'the focus on behaviour; the attention to symptoms; the importance of the role of the group and the value of the knowledge and experience of the "oldtimers" [long-time members]; and the viewing of the problem [alcoholism] as chronic [the alcoholic is viewed as never being cured]' (Gartner and Riessman, 1977, p. 25). The controlling tendencies of Alcoholics Anonymous – mutual surveillance by members and public concern about, if not actual punishment of, backsliders – are found in many other Anonymous groups. Such groups are concerned invariably with working within accepted societal norms to change the behaviour of individuals. In AA the individual is expected to be guided by the Twelve Steps and the Twelve Traditions which express the principles on which the groups are run.

The fact that the ideology of AA has found its way into several of the other larger Anonymous organisations is not surprising because Gamblers Anonymous, Narcotics Anonymous and Neurotics Anonymous were founded by members of AA and have accepted the Twelve Steps and the Twelve Traditions on which their work is based (Gartner and Riessman, 1977, pp. 29–31).

Groups for relatives and carers Many groups have been set up to deal with the special circumstances and difficulties which can arise for people who are living with somebody with a need or problem. For example, in community care self-help groups offer an indirect form of support for those with needs or problems, through the help given directly to the carer, who may be a friend or relative.

The groups may run in partnership with an existing group which caters directly for the person experiencing the problem. An example is Al-Anon, for relatives and friends of someone with a drink problem, who may be a member of an AA group. The nature of this sort of support group, sometimes called a 'living-with group', is affected greatly by the extent of dependence on the carer of the person with the problem. The carer of an elderly confused relative who is doubly incontinent, or for a baby, may have to cope with a much greater intensity of round-the-clock involvement in the task and the impact on her or him may be much greater.

The living-with group quite often caters for members trying to cope with people who share similar conditions. Initial contact with such a group is likely to provide the newcomer with the reassurance of meeting someone who previously has been through similar conditions. It will probably also provide her or him with much needed information about the condition, from the standpoint of the carer. Parents who get together because they have children suffering from the same illness may thus share experiences, from their first awareness that something was wrong, to the present day.

Self-help therapy groups   There is a vast variety of self-help groups with a therapeutic orientation. However, it is in the area of feminist therapy groups that some of the most exciting, and paradoxical, features of self-help can be seen. Feminist therapy reflects the influence of feminism on psychotherapy and unsurprisingly its principal focus is on the impact of sexism on the problems of individual women. Importantly, the attention is paid to sexism as one aspect of the social structure (Howell, 1981, p. 512). To that extent, feminist therapy no less than much psychotherapy acknowledges the social dimension of problems which seem to be located within the individual.

The feminist therapy group may be represented as one type of consciousness-raising. But to the extent that consciousness-raising is concerned with social and political – or at any rate extra-psychic – change, the activity of therapy may be absent from it altogether (Howell, 1981, p. 510). With regard to feminist therapy groups, a more subtle and challenging issue emerges. If we accept that fundamental to the feminist viewpoint is the preoccupation with the socially-based rather than individually-based explanation of a person's symptoms, then the likelihood is that the feminist will regard as suspect any hint that the causes of a problem lie in individual pathology. We may thus find that feminist therapy which rejects psychodynamic discussion of the origins of, and responses to, problems resembles consciousness-raising since it is likely to assert the need for social change and political action.

Groups for people experiencing stigma AA is but one expression of an enthusiasm for self-help which has a fervour drawn in part from moral crusades to improve the lot of people experiencing stigma. In the politicisation of HIV/AIDS we can detect a hardening of attitudes towards the victim of the condition, which perhaps heightens the moralistic tone of official responses. But the self-help groups and organisations which grew in response to HIV/AIDS differ from AA. Whereas AA itself has taken on some of the moral values of society in relation to drink problems, self-help HIV/AIDS groups, if anything, set themselves against such moralistic attitudes.

In the 1980s, HIV/AIDS became a focus of self-help activity. In a way, this illustrates a tendency of governments and officials to push the responsibility for developing the condition on to individuals. HIV/AIDS at first was perceived by many people as a consequence of the lifestyle of the individual rather than as a matter for public health. HIV/AIDS has been described mistakenly as the 'gay plague'. Implicitly, there is an assumption that to catch HIV/AIDS is to demonstrate perverted or immoral habits, such as homosexuality or promiscuity. Growing concern about the spread of HIV/AIDS to the heterosexual population may have contributed to enhanced public funding of many initiatives and research programmes, though there may be a tension between meeting the goal of benefiting HIV/AIDS sufferers and serving the profit motive of some drug producers.

Taken in the context of a general tendency for government to contract public health services to private and voluntary providers and to encourage self-help in the context of an enhanced voluntary sector, it is not surprising that self-help is growing in the HIV/AIDS field. More important, perhaps, this is an illustration of the role self-help plays in areas of life where prejudice and moral panics rule over tolerance and rationality.

In the US, a well-known self-help organisation, New York Gay Men's Health Crisis (GMHC), was founded in 1981 by forty men whose friends or lovers had HIV/AIDS. Although its members sought services to help them, they seem to have soon found that they had to take action to help themselves (Altman, 1986, p. 84). In 1982, the HIV/AIDS Foundation developed from its base in California into a national organisation, involved in educational and lobbying activities (Altman, 1986, p. 88). In general, in countries where gay organisations flourish and have strong links with government, HIV/AIDS self-help has tended to develop around them. This has happened in Canada, Denmark and the Netherlands. In Britain also, after Terrence Higgins died from HIV/AIDS, the Terrence Higgins Trust (THT) was founded in 1982, modelled largely on the GMHC. By mid-1985, the THT had over 250 volunteers (Altman, 1986, p. 91). Gay organisations have mobilised and grown in strength around health issues such as HIV/AIDS in much the same way that many feminist groups have focused upon issues concerned with women's health. But this does not mean that self-help is the preserve exclusively of gay groups, or of men or women. Yet it is a reflection of the way HIV/AIDS has had an impact on the gay community, in increasing its cohesion and solidarity.

Self-development

Self-development includes a wide variety of activities with an educational, social and personal development focus, including Peer Self-Help Psychotherapy Groups (PSHPG) and Integrity Groups which have spread widely throughout the US. It also includes a great range of gender-associated health groups in Britain.

Peer self-help psychotherapy groups may or may not be affiliated to the national network of the same name, and their local practices, such as frequency of meeting, vary widely. Their focus varies also, from quite major shared problems of addiction or neurosis to the general area of personal development. It has been noted that these groups are not without a number of the difficulties which beset self-help groups generally: the development of cliques, disruption to group activities by individual members who are feeling upset or disturbed, exploitation of the lonely and distressed by predatory group members and the reinforcement of problems by an over-emphasis on problems and bad experiences in meetings (Hurvitz, 1974, p. 93). As Hurvitz says: 'Most people with a problem that defines a particular group never attend a PSHGP meeting, despite the considerably publicity some of these groups receive' (1974, p. 92).

Integrity groups exemplify the way some such activities cross the boundary between problem-focusing and self-development. Integrity Groups operate in the US and illustrate a well-established and structured approach to self-help in mental health. The groups run according to detailed guidelines which are open enough to allow a variety of practice. Members have to commit themselves to three principles: honesty, responsibility and involvement in group proceedings.

Gender-associated groups Although the women's movement is particularly visible and influential in the field of self-help and health, this is not to suggest that the issues of gender should be addressed only in that area. Clearly, gender issues affect the entire field of self-help. Though women self-helpers may be described as benefiting from the support offered by a group, this is an experience many men also seek. Increasingly, gender-based groups tackle men's issues, including different perspectives on different masculinities.

The nature of gender-linked groups has been influenced by feminism and by the way the women's movement has highlighted the oppression of women in general, in the workplace, the home, education, leisure and other activities. It also confronts gender inequalities in the practice of professionals such as doctors, teachers and social workers. It is unavoidable that challenges by women to the masculine biases in the study of culture and society (Rowbotham *et al.* 1980, p. 55), and in the power relations reflected in them, tend to be reflected by the illustrations here of women's groups. This should not be regarded complacently as inevitable or proper, but as one sign of male power over the everyday construction of knowledge of self-help and empowerment.

Gender-associated groups illustrate the impossibility of segregating self-help activities concerned with problems or self-development from the concerns of consciousness-raising. Women's groups include those concerned with health, therapy and consciousness-raising. However, some women writers about Women's Liberation Groups distinguish these from therapy groups, by the fact that the latter promote solutions to the problems of individual women while the former are based on the principle that solutions for individual women depend first on changes in the conditions in which all women live their lives (Zweig, 1971, p. 161).

Health groups Health groups may be viewed by members as educating them out of their socialisation in professionally dominated situations. Groups may set out to reveal ways in which the health professions shelter behind displays of professional knowledge and skill. Such groups tend to contradict the consumerism of market-based community care. They represent a public approach to health rather than a private contract to cure (Chamberlain, 1981, p. 155). Groups may thus be able to resist dominant social attitudes and may act politically to tackle health issues.

Women's health groups are concerned more broadly with the struggle for autonomy, the right to choose, make decisions and exercise control over what happens to their bodies. Women's health groups typically comprise eight or nine members meeting regularly to exchange experiences and knowledge about their bodies, feelings, attitudes and problems. While members discuss some matters of particular concern to women, such as pregnancy, menstruation and some cancers, they may be concerned also with more general health issues. Women's health groups may be based on holistic principles, having regard to a person's needs in relation to the entire environment.

Consciousness-raising (CR)

This may focus on benefit to the individual, but in such settings as women's health groups or community action groups, it may take on a social change character. To the extent that feminist therapy reflects the influence of feminism on psychotherapy, the concern of such groups is partly problem-focused and partly on sexism as one aspect of the social structure (Howell, 1981, p. 512). Self-help groups involving women cover a wide range of areas, from specific gynaecological topics to general health or consciousness raising. However, Marieskind's point that most are primarily educational and concerned with enabling individuals to realise their potential (Marieskind, 1984, p. 28), should not deflect out attention from the tensions between problem-focused and consciousness-raising self-help activities.

Survivors' groups Survivors' groups form a powerful and growing force in the field of mental health reform. But in the fields of mental health and disability, professionals and carers still may disempower people by doing their participating and self-helping for them. One illustration of the upsurge of consumer-led self-advocacy is the growth of organised survivors' groups. Survivors' groups have spread through the developed countries and include former patients, such as people who have been in mental hospitals. Some have well-established networks of contact people, furthered in some cases by magazines or newsletters. 'Survivors Speak Out', for example, the networking organisation (see Chapter 4) helps individuals and groups to keep in touch with each other and encourages self-advocacy. Another example is the development of groups by and for women who have experienced sexual and other forms of abuse.

Self-advocacy Self-advocacy is becoming increasingly important in some fields of self-help, notably mental health. Co-operatives for people with physical and mental disabilities, linked with self-advocacy, are becoming more common as people seek more imaginative ways of promoting self-help among those experiencing a range of disabilities. These latter developments reflect attempts to move towards the democratisation of social work services and have helped to give social workers the impetus to explore ways of working alongside consumer groups in the health and social services in the 1990s. This is partly as a result of the growing strength of consumer-led movements generally. One consequence has been a trend towards some professionals acknowledging that many people have the capacity to do things for themselves, but need empowering in order to achieve them.

The essential elements of consciousness-raising in the self-help field which are worth noting at this stage include their critical stance in relation to the services people receive, and the innovative and (from the viewpoint of the bureaucrat) often untidy and unruly character of groups and organisations. Yet, this is the vital, energising and creative force which gives this area of self-help so much of its momentum, from which social workers have so much to learn and to gain.

Process of group-based empowerment

Three stages seem to be common to many self-help and user-led groups: initiation, self-movement and proselytising. Caution needs to be exercised about how rigidly the general analysis of stages is applied to particular groups. Some commentators have produced very detailed checklists of the stages groups go through. In general, the more specific and detailed the checklist, the more caution has to be exercised about applying it to the vast range of specific situations. For example, Mullender and Ward detail five major stages, breaking down into twelve steps, in their model of self-directed groupwork. But they caution that 'we would not suggest that what actually happens in practice is as neatly tied and labelled as such an account may imply, nor that anyone should try to force reality to conform to the stages and steps of the model. One way of conceptualising the framework is as a grid, upon which can be placed all our ideas and actions in a piece of work, thus enabling us to see them in relation one to another, rather than in a linear progression' (Mullender and Ward, 1991, pp. 18–19).

Initiation

Initiation or entry entails starting an activity or breaking into an existing one. A variety of significant elements may be associated with the start of the process, to do with the preparations an individual makes, such as admitting that an issue or problem has reached the point where something needs to be done about it. At this point, the person may desire to join a group or find someone with whom to share the experience. During this period a new group may be set up, or an agreement may be reached between a new member and an existing group, about how the group may be useful and what she or he may bring to it.

Self-movement

The idea of self-movement is used here to include a wide range of activities, all of which involve a self-sustaining element. This may be problem-centred, socialisation or growth-centred, self-development or training-centred, con-sciousness-raising or social action-centred.

We can be more specific. For instance, in the problem-cen-tred and problem-solving areas, the focus may be upon *change*. Change may be anticipated at different levels and is not confined to interpersonal change. It may involve conversion or healing, what Sarbin and Alder (1971, p. 606) call the anni-hilation and reconstruction of the self. Or, less melodramati-`cally, certain behaviour may cease and other behaviour take its place. Conversion may be stimulated by trigger mechan-isms, or by the use of a structure such as the public confession which forms a part of many problem-centred self-help groups. This happens in a good many of the anonymous groups mod-elled on AA, but it may be present also in the personal state-ment required of a member of a consciousness-raising group. Healing, or some other form of help, may be made avail-able to an individual by other members of the group by means of mechanisms like acceptance. Acceptance may sound akin to forgiveness, although as happens in AA groups, heal-ing may lie a long way from the self-reliance or mutual aid of other groups, since in AA, responsibility for healing and for-giveness is located with God as ultimate, extra-group auth-ority. Again, the cost of cure may be seen in quasi-religious terms to involve some act of penance, as may happen in AA. The member may be expected to go through the disempower-ing experience of baring his or her soul in the group, in the struggle towards the empowerment of gaining control over the drink problem.

Proselytising

In a further – possibly final – proselytising stage, the individual moves on to help others. It is a mistake to see this as necessarily following conversion, since there are circumstances where a person repeatedly moves from one to the other and back again. Or the two processes of helping others and being helped may proceed simultaneously. Finally, of course, a person may look outside the group and may even advertise the positive impact of the experience by recruiting others, or may leave the activity to start a fresh one.

People in different situations encounter very different issues as they go through the process of self-help. Thus, members of Weightwatchers may be able to share their successes proudly with others, whereas members of more stigmatised groups may feel driven to be more circumspect. In the latter case, members of AA may share similar problems of re-acceptance by others as some former mental patients. In the past, AA has tried to counter this by using the allergy concept of alcoholism, which assumes that people develop drink problems because of a physiological predisposition over which they have no control. In this way, AA members could be viewed as sick rather than as mentally ill or as blameworthy. One consequence could be that the presumption that the drinker is merely an allergic victim of alcohol may lead simply to the eventual release of the non-drinker from the deviant label of alcoholic. Or, the outcome could be that problem drinking becomes seen as behaviour over which some people have no control.

In contrast, the experience of a consciousness-raising group is likely to be more overtly empowering, by being more educationally than problem-focused:

A CR group decides to look at the topic of education. From the discussion of their personal experiences the women learn that many of them were interested in the sciences but were not encouraged to pursue their interest. They go on to look at how the fields of science are dominated by men who were actively encouraged at school to continue their education. The women learn something about the limits imposed by sex-role stereotyping in education. (Donnan and Lenton, 1985, p. 17)

In the next chapter, we consider the issues encountered in group-based empowerment-in-practice.

6

Empowering Groups: Implementation

Introduction

This chapter examines group-based empowerment-in-practice. The lack of examples in Chapter 5, of practice which illustrate how groupwork empowers, is redressed to an extent in this chapter. It also uses examples from practice as a means of exploring issues which arise.

How does empowerment start?

Several factors are involved in the process of getting empowerment started and ensuring its effective continuance, either for a limited period or on an open-ended basis.

Finding enough group members

Enough members need to be found to start an activity, yet a way may need to be found of attracting only those whose purposes are consonant with the intended activity. This begs crucial questions about mechanisms to screen potential participants in activities, whether these should exist and if so how they should be set up (Donnan and Lenton, 1985, p. 44). How far should the professional intervene in a facilitated or autonomous user-led or self-help group? It also raises the issue as to whether groups should have open or closed membership. Open groups generally allow new members to join at any time, while closed groups allow no more members to join after they have reached an agreed size. The screening process may be either formal or informal. Formal procedures may involve discussions or meetings between founding or existing participants. Intending participants may be given information about the group's activities as a whole or about other participants and in return may be expected to provide some information. The choice as to whether to attend may be left with the new participant or be made in a meeting by all the existing participants. The existing participants may accept new participants once and for all, or in the case of some therapeutically-oriented groups may require each to go through a number of probationary or trial meetings.

In general, the more restrictions the existing participants impose on potential group members, the more limited is the pool of potential participants. However, the very need for members to retain a sharp focus on a narrowly defined task may necessitate the insistence on an entry requirement, as in the case of a women's group dealing with sexual abuse or rape, which excludes professionals and men.

Finding a place to meet

Undoubtedly, the participation of people in self-help or user-led activities depends initially on adequate publicity being given to planned events and subsequently on the establishment of effective means of communication. In some instances, groups rely on word-of-mouth communication once meetings have become routinised. Others produce newsletters where membership of an organisation or group is more scattered and activities do not necessarily take the form of face-to-face group meetings. The use of a variety of media may improve the image of an activity and enable potential participants, the general public and professionals such as social workers to receive information about it. Robinson and

Henry's study of self-help groups in the health field, based on members' own accounts, identifies three factors as important in their origins: the failure of existing services, the recognition of the value of mutual help, and the role of the media (Robinson and Henry, 1977, p. 12).

The issue of successful publicity is inseparable from that of resources. It may be necessary to produce posters, advertisements, leaflets or newspaper articles before a core of active participants has been generated, who would be able to help to resource them. We have seen in Chapter 5 how the social worker may use the publicity arising from the typical experience of an individual, either in a newspaper article or a leaflet, to raise public concern when a local group is being founded.

Guaranteeing adequate support

Bond notes the usefulness of a notice board which helps to support local groups as well as promoting the entire organisation. But the group he is studying may be unusually structured, for he describes the notice board as displaying guidelines, training and opportunities for contacts with more established chapters, by which he means other local groups. His example is a federated structure of local groups within an established framework. As he says:

> The corporate structure also provides public relations information, organises workshops and conducts the national convention, providing broader opportunities for all members to become involved in the large-scale development of the organisation. (Bond *et al.*, 1979, p. 60)

But while a corporate structure may be a bonus for some groups, many flourish without it. Indeed, there is something to be said for an organisation which is loose enough for each local group to develop an autonomous local identity, purely as a reflection of its members' interests, preferences and needs.

Achieving legitimacy

'Legitimacy' concerns the credibility or acceptability of an activity in the eyes of relevant people, including professionals and other members, where appropriate. The group Bond studied gained legitimacy through the active support of professionals such as doctors.

The way a self-help or user-led group is run is crucial to its maintenance. Knight and Hayes (1981, pp. 83–4) suggest that social and recreational activities may help to improve the credibility of a self-help or user-led group with potential members. Local people should also be involved in the management, to the extent of employing them alongside other professionals wherever possible.

All self-help or user-led activities need to maintain a degree of credibility both with existing and potential participants. Clearly, acceptability to professionals is not a requirement for every group's survival. In instances of a self-help or user-led group functioning as complementary with professional services, the sympathy or support of professionals may be valuable. Where the group operates as an alternative to, or as competitor with, existing services, distance from professionals will of necessity be maintained.

Support from professionals makes a positive difference. Unell observes that 100 per cent of new initiatives given professional support in the Nottingham Self-help Project led to groups being established, in contrast with about 40 per cent of those given limited or no support (Unell, 1987, p. 37). However, these may have been a self-defining sample of groups needing some facilitation. On the whole, an autonomous self-help or user-led group gains its legitimacy either independently of professionals, or by contrasting itself with them. It is important for social workers not to deny to group members this right to distinguish themselves clearly from the aura of professional practice.

Recruiting helpers

In the group Bond studied, the recruitment process was helped particularly by existing members visiting potential new members in connection with the serious surgical operations that were being carried out on them.

The success of initiatives often depends largely on the ability of participants to make connections at the right pace and at the appropriate time, between people who would form supportive chains in aspects crucial to the survival of these projects.

Potential members of groups and organisations may be thought to be mainly articulate and middle-class. But this varies very much from setting to setting. Some organisations, like the Humberside Project (see Chapter 7), recruit predominately working-class participants by virtue of their location. Others find that their membership covers a wide social class spectrum. In an admittedly small-scale survey of mental health self-help or user-led groups associated with the Mind Your Self project in 1984, it was noted that in one group a university researcher took part alongside semi-skilled and unskilled unemployed members (Lindenfield and Adams, 1984, pp. 24–5).

Nevertheless, somehow at the start, activities need a push. As Knight and Hayes (1981, p. 88) put it: 'To get started groups need highly motivated, articulate and numerate individuals to hold frequent meetings to mount campaigns of action.'

Mullender and Ward categorise membership of self-directed groups in terms of empowering features and those which are disempowering, most of which factors are within the control of group members. Disempowering features include the limitation of membership by selection processes; the deterrence of members from joining because race and gender issues are ignored; closed and compulsory membership imposed by the worker. Empowering features include open, voluntary membership with no limit on the size of the group; advertisement of the group and clear signals to black members and women members that they will not experience racism or sexism in the group (Mullender and Ward, 1991, p. 60).

Maintaining involvement

Self-help or user-led groups need to involve sufficient participants to enable the programme to proceed. The impetus of each activity will be improved to the extent that participants have a personal stake in it. Whilst the success of a programme as a whole may be problematic in the sense that it remains a matter of opinion and experience, the maintenance of each activity depends on more objective criteria such as a certain minimum level of attendance and participation by members.

The circumstances of newcomers to groups are similar in some ways to those of new volunteers in social welfare organisations, who originally seek personal help but more often than not shift to getting satisfaction from helping others (Katz, 1970, p. 60). In other words, people participate in a group because they are getting something out of it. In the early stages, recruits may receive more than they contribute, whilst later on the balance between help received and help given may be rather different.

The effectiveness of involvement of participants depends on how well activities are managed. Group meetings in particular need effective leaders (Lindenfield and Adams, 1984, p. 33). On the whole, a democratic style of leadership is preferable to authoritarian or laissez-faire approaches (Lindenfield and Adams, 1984, pp. 34–5). Some people argue that larger groups benefit from having two or more leaders working together, but Preston-Shoot considers this too simplistic and examines the conditions under which it would be appropriate (Preston-Shoot, 1987, ch. 4).

More substantial advice on running meetings can be found in handbooks such as that by Holloway and Otto (1986).

Integrity Groups have also produced guidelines for the conduct of effective group meetings (Mowrer, 1972, p. 27).

It is tidy, but misleading, to assume that self-help groups' activities are coterminus with the total of members' self-help and self-care. It is quite common to find members developing relationships within their group, which generate a variety of extra-group activities. In informal, social, leisure and other areas, relationships, projects and friendships develop out of meetings, sustain them and are sustained by them.

It is a short step from this process to consider the notion that groups may be open-ended rather than time limited. In contrast with many contract-linked therapeutic areas of a more formal or traditional nature, self-help or user-led activities generally do not have the same concern with limited involvement in the helping process. By the same token, members of a group may not set their sights so much on total cure or release from problems as the outcome of activities, as upon the week-by-week management of those problems as the group proceeds. In other words, membership of a particular group may become a way of life.

Associated with this broadening of relationships between group members, is the issue of confidentiality. Some self-help or user-led groups actually have rules forbidding members to discuss business relating to the group outside the meetings. This underlines the need for participants to clarify the boundaries of their relationships with, and responsibilities to, each other.

Securing sufficient resources

Self-help and user-led groups and organisations draw their resources from a wide variety of sources. Some larger organisations seek and obtain large grants from statutory bodies, national or locally.

Advice on getting grants is succinctly expressed by a joint working party of the Association of Metropolitan Authorities (AMA), the National Council for Voluntary Organisations (NCVO) and the Association of County Councils (ACC)

(Jones, 1981, chs 2–4). Advice on such contracts contains sufficient arguments in favour of them to overcome most of the doubts of the faint-hearted (Jones, 1981, pp. 9–11) and there is a model contract in appendix 5 of Jones (1981). One particularly useful tip from the working party concerns the advantages of leaving the detailed scheduling of activities out of the document, so that these can be modified separately without affecting the overall agreement, in subsequent reviews (Jones, 1981, p. 10). Obviously, such written agreements do not in themselves resolve issues which have not been sorted out elsewhere. As the working party conclude: 'Contracts themselves do not create mutual trust. Rather they are the products of such trust' (Jones, 1981, p. 11).

The relevance of agreements lies in their public relations value to group members who need to establish credibility with potential sources of resources, of whatever kind. They demonstrate to other people the capacity to relate positively and easily and the capacity to work effectively with professionals, and subsequently they may even be used to show that the resources and effort have been used in a worthwhile way. The features of successful consultation arrangements between statutory and voluntary bodies have been noted by the working party referred to above (Jones, 1981, pp. 28–9).

Money is not the sole, or even the main, resource for the small, local self-help or user-led group, which may depend on having somewhere to meet and the facilities to make tea or coffee during meetings. A minimum of administrative support, such as the means of making posters or leaflets, may be vital also to enable the group to get started. The location of meetings may be crucial, for the setting greatly influences the tone of meetings. Some self-help or user-led groups will have the offer of subsidised or free accommodation; some will meet in members' homes to avoid any contact with professional premises; others will hire a room to ensure meetings take place as far as possible on neutral territory.

Caution should be exercised wherever possible to ensure safeguards against loss of resourcing. For instance, self-help or user-led groups or organisations may grow to the point where they seem self-supporting. In other words, service users and professionals involved with them need to appreciate the risks of becoming too successful in other people's eyes.

How should group members handle difficulties?

A number of difficulties may arise in the running of self-help and user groups and organisations. We can see such problems generally in terms of the power struggles which go on in such circumstances: people vying for attention and for control, within themselves and between one another.

Conceptualisations of group processes may underplay references to problems and crises which can be so major as to lead to the premature demise of an activity. It is worth noting that participants in activities need the necessary knowledge and skills to enable them to deal with such areas as people whose problems tend to dominate and exclude consideration of other essential matters. Additionally, participants in activities may need to be able to cope with each other's sadness as well as anger and, in extreme circumstances, even violence (Lindenfield and Adams, 1984, ch. 5: Preston-Shoot, 1987, pp. 105–10). Furthermore, some self-help or user-led initiatives can be put at risk by the tendency for an individual or small clique to dominate a group or organisation. Difficulties may be evident in the form of leadership problems, personality clashes and all the multitude of niggling hiccups which seem to beset meetings and activities in any group from time to time. Other participants need to possess the necessary skills to assert control in such circumstances and maintain the purpose of the activity.

Conflict or disruption? An issue of power?

There is a need for all to take responsibility for the social health of the group or organisation. As far as possible, members should strive to maintain a healthy balance between tolerating creative imbalances of power, conflicts and clashes and keeping them within reasonable limits. It is important not to see conflict necessarily as a sign that all is not well in the group. Many groups thrive on conflict. The important thing is for participants to ensure that other people feel they are gaining something from the meetings and other activities.

But however creative conflict is, it can be very harmful if it is not dealt with effectively when it arises. On the whole, it is usually more helpful than not for conflicts to be brought out into the open by means of members sharing their different feelings and views.

The response to disruptive individuals should also be neither to ignore them nor to panic! Usually, the reason for the behaviour of the person who disrupts by talking too much, interrupting or shouting, becoming aggressive or violent, can be seen quite quickly, if we ask ourselves the question 'why are they seeking attention/exercising power in this way?'

Sometimes it is sufficient for the meeting to be suspended while time is given to this person. The time spent can be repaid by them settling down quickly. Others may need to talk about their feelings outside the meeting. Some may decide that these meetings are not for them. It is important for the social worker, as it is for other members, to accept that the activity is not beneficial to everybody. Some people may need counselling out of it.

It is important also to recognise that disruption to the activity should not necessarily be seen as though it is the responsibility of one person. There is a danger in self-help and user groups, as in all groups, of one person becoming the butt of the bad feelings of others. This scapegoated person may be perceived as disruptive when in fact there are imbalances in the way other people are relating to each other, which may need serious and careful examination before proceeding further.

Apathy or non-participation

The reciprocal of the symptomatic disruptiveness referred to above is apathetic behaviour by one or more members. This may take the form of silence, non-participation or simply staying away from meetings. In many ways, everything we have said about handling aggressive behaviour or conflict situations applies here. However, it is always worth bearing in mind that the situation can be improved dramatically, simply by introducing some new stimulation into the meeting, such as an exercise involving physical movement, or a social break for people to make hot drinks and chat for a while. The handling of conflict by members of groups is dealt with in Lindenfield and Adams (1984, ch. 5) and that between organisations in Jones (1981, pp. 35–6).

Participants need their quota of resilience to deal with difficulties like these, as well as with the ultimate problem of the failure of an activity, not losing hope but restarting and continuing.

How is a self-help or user-led group maintained?

Sourcebooks for practice

There are many handbooks which offer step-by-step advice to initiators of self-help or user-led groups. For instance, Donnan and Lenton (1985) have written for individual women as well as for group facilitators, Phyllis Silverman (1980) has rooted her advice in research as well as personal experience, and Judy Wilson has discussed the practicalities of self-help (1986) and carers' (1988) groups in Britain. In fifteen perceptive pages, Liz Evans *et al.* (1986, chs 6 and 7) give advice to carers such as parents of disabled children on setting up and running self-help groups. Mullender and Ward target their book specifically at workers involved in user-led groups (Mullender and Ward, 1991).

Facilitating empowerment-in-practice

Regardless of the setting, the major empowering role for the worker is likely to be as a facilitator. The facilitator acts as a consultant rather than as leader of the group. Facilitation involves bringing people together in the first instance and supporting them subsequently. In her study of the Nottingham Self-Help project, Judith Unell identifies six elements which are inherent in support of self-help: the direct provision of practical resources, the provision of access to practical resources elsewhere, putting people in touch with each other, creating opportunities for different groups to keep in touch and meet, promoting the idea of self-help among professionals and giving new groups specific help (Unell, 1987, pp. 6–7).

In facilitating self-help or user-led groups, the role of the social worker may be summarised as follows:

1. establishing at the outset a boundary rather than a central role for the social worker
2. not taking the lead in determining the focus, the pace of activity, the goals or the means of getting there
3. standing alongside the group members rather than above them in terms of power, skills and professional activity
4. acting as someone who is available to be consulted rather than as an imposed, supervisory presence.

Example

Starting point: identifying the need for action   June is a social worker who has worked in conjunction with a voluntary organisation concerned with mental health and has become aware of the number of phone calls received from people wanting help of various kinds. The difficulty is that callers asking for advice about depression, tranquillisers, phobias and so on invariably do not want to give an address for information to be sent and tend not to ring back for a further chat with a worker. In one or two cases, people have been given information, including invitations to come to chat to a worker.

June talks it over with colleagues in the voluntary organisation and they decide to mobilise a self-help group. Drawing on experience gained from similar initiatives in mental health, they follow a series of stages designed to maximise support to people who may become involved, with particular regard to empowering participants.

Determining how to respond June and members of the local voluntary organisation take a number of considered and purposeful decisions based on their estimate of the need which exists and information they collate. Together with their previous experience, this points towards the potential benefit of facilitating a group. Before acting, they agree on the principles to which they are committed, which will be reflected in any decisions they take subsequently. This is important to them because at this stage they cannot anticipate in detail what might happen, although they have certain expectations.

The decision to facilitate a group follows partly from the picture gained of a typical caller with a problem, who is worried enough to contact the agency but apparently has not the confidence to follow it up. It follows also from experience of one of the workers in the voluntary organisation, who was a member of a group which failed. She shares this experience with June, who correlates it with what she has read.

It appears that half a dozen people who were trying to cope with various mental health problems, the most common being depression, accepted an invitation to meet and talk regularly with each other, but that after a couple of meetings only two were left and then the group collapsed altogether.

June and her colleagues take action to ensure that their facilitated group learns from these experiences. This involves offering to people invited to join a group a clear agreement that a measure of support will be provided at the outset with the *resources* entailed in setting up and maintaining the group, accompanied by specific help with the development of the *skills* members will need to run meetings.

Settling the purpose of the group   The *value base and goals* of the group can be defined for its potential members even before it has its first meeting, so as to enable them to manage their own problems. To that end, June ensures right from the start that everyone realises her role is to get the group going. Subsequently, she will withdraw to a position of marginal involvement from which she can service the group if members call upon her. The issue of the group's value base may raise difficulties, since the worker's role is to facilitate, not to impose. It will be necessary to act as consultant to the group, rather than to direct this process. It is a matter of judgement for the worker to decide, for example, whether, and if so how long, to work with a group some of whose practices are not consistent with anti-oppressive practice. Again, the worker will need to decide how to challenge such practices. Mullender and Ward have set out useful general guidelines for this (Mullender and Ward, 1991, pp. 30–1).

Planning and programming   The steps June and her colleagues take include finding a suitable room for meetings to take place and ensuring that it is reasonably comfortable and has access to a power point for the making of refreshments. Given the feelings of many callers about their experiences as clients, the decision is taken to use a room in the building housing the local Council for Voluntary Service. Rent will have to be paid from some source if the group continues, but for the initial meetings this and other expenses are met from agency funds. The meeting room thus is on *neutral territory*, which may be crucial to people who have experienced the stigma of being clients or patients.

A number of advertisements are placed in local shop windows and agency offices, inviting people to an initial meeting; also the meeting is mentioned to callers where appropriate. Articles   carefully   placed   by   arrangement   with

sympathetic journalists, in the columns of local news-
papers dealing with voluntary organisations and activities
using pen sketches of typical problems, may prove productive.

At the *first meeting*, June and her colleague from the voluntary organisation take steps to defuse people's fears as they arrive. Coffee, tea and biscuits are provided and people
introduce themselves to each other. A short series of meetings
may be planned, after people's expectations and fears have
been shared. June makes sure that she offers sufficient support in this process to hold the group together. She antici-
pates that the needs of the group in its early stages will be for
adequate leadership and the *acquisition of skills* and techniques to
enable its objectives to be determined and worked towards.

Developing rules and procedures In the early meetings, June
and her colleague from the voluntary organisation help the
members to draw up a number of *simple rules*. These clarify
whether the group is open-ended, how often it will meet, how
long each meeting runs, what the pattern of activities is and
so on. From experience, she knows that reaching agreement
about these can take time.

Of course, there is no reason why a particular structured and
formalised system of rules should be worked out. But it often
helps to see an example of what somebody else has used in
practice, even if this serves only to reinforce one's prior conclusion that it would be better not to set up anything in advance.
Justification for the latter is provided by those who prefer to
leave it to the group to arrive at its own collective decisions, completely unaided. However, for those who prefer the former
approach, an example of the kinds of rules which can operate
is provided by Integrity Groups, mentioned in Chapter 5, for
which the 15 guidelines paraphrased below provide a helpful basis for working out the kinds of guidelines which may
apply in a particular case, even if they serve only to stimulate the
reader to depart from the extremely rigid controls they em-
body:

1. Any member threatening or carrying out physical violence against people or things may be summarily expelled.
2. Anyone walking out during the process of working through a problem or feeling will be judged to have resigned permanently from the group.
3. Anyone can use *any* language or wordless sounds during a group meeting.
4. Sub-grouping, that is whispering to one's neighbour, is not allowed.
5. Non-attenders should notify the group in advance, giving their reasons.
6. Late attenders who do not warn the group in advance may be asked to explain their lateness.
7. Discussions between members on group matters between group meetings should be reported at the next group meeting, though such friendships are encouraged.
8. Members who tell each other's stories outside group meetings to non-members may be expelled for breaching confidentiality.
9. Members are free to leave after three hours of a meeting, even though it has not finished.
10. Any member can leave a meeting, but would be encouraged to talk about it first.
11. If the group cannot meet members' needs in normal weekly meetings, then extra meetings may be called.
12. If an individual feels he or she is not making progress, or a crisis arises, then an extra meeting may be called by her or him to deal with this.
13. The task of chairperson circulates at meetings and should be carried out flexibly and inventively.
14. Someone who has a grievance against a different group's member, after discussion in the group, should seek the chance of taking it up with that person in the other group.
15. Communities with two or more Integrity Groups may exchange members between groups every few months (Mowrer, 1972, pp. 26–7).

perience and finish their contact with an agency, group or organisation there and then. Both for individuals and groups, there is a need to consider endings as a common and natural stage in the process of the group. Endings involve a transition to another kind of activity. This needs stating more strongly in the face of the tendency for self-help and user groups to often be more open-ended and ongoing than some other forms of helping based upon professional resources. But, ironically, it also needs emphasising for the opposite reason that many group-based initiatives are short-lived, for all kinds of reasons (Lindenfield and Adams, 1984, pp. 53–5). Finally, we should avoid assuming that there is some inbuilt normative rationality about such endings, which makes everything always turn out for the best. The reasons for the closure of a group are various and complex:

> It may have achieved what its members set out for it to achieve, it may want to amalgamate with another group, it may be prevented from further meetings, or the interaction between members may lead to its prompt, even sudden, closure. (Lindenfield and Adams, 1984, p. 55)

Three types of ending are mentioned here, from which different permutations of individual and collective ending can be extended:

(a) The end of the activity or meeting Essentially, this ending should not come as a surprise to any of its participants and all should have the chance to prepare for it in advance. The more some sort of structure is adhered to, with pre-set starting and finishing times for meetings, the more likely it is that members will be able to anticipate the ending and retain control of their situation in the process. It helps if one or more members who are sharing leadership roles in the activity can take on the task of bringing explicitly to people's attention the fact that the meeting will be finishing in, say, ten minutes' time.

The actual closing of the meeting can be preceded with some form of stocktaking activity. It may be sufficient to go round the entire group asking for comments. Or a more structured exercise may be preferred, with members writing one good and one bad feeling about what has happened on pieces of paper, which are folded and put into a box, then taken out, read and discussed without identifying the author of each. The latter course can be frustrating if sufficient time is not allowed to read out and talk about all the slips of paper.

(b) *Where the individual wishes to end her or his contact with the self-help or user group or organisation*   The conditions in which people stop taking part vary tremendously. Some attend but overtly do not seem to participate, then stop attending with no warning or explanation. Others announce their intentions in advance. All that can be done here is to note that if members announce their intentions in advance, then clearly this signals the appropriateness of a response from the other members.

First, it may be productive to check out with the individual whether she or he wants to talk about the reason for leaving. The motive for saying 'I am leaving' may have to do with attracting the attention of other people. There may be some personal reason, such as an emergency or trauma, illness or accident. There may be a conflict with another group member. Sadness or unhappiness may contribute to the wish to withdraw. Any of these may need dealing with by other members of the group. The effectiveness of the activity at such times depends on those participating maintaining a sufficiently secure and supportive atmosphere to enable the issues to be explored and worked through.

(c) *Where the group or organisation is closing*   A surprisingly high proportion of self-help or user-led groups and organisations cease after a few meetings. It is important for the social worker to reassure people that this is normal and desirable, as long as members themselves desire it! Self-help or user-led groups can come to an end because they have run their course, members have dropped away, most members feel the activities have achieved their objectives or people are joining other groups or organisations.

In all such circumstances, it may make sense to try to mark the occasion in some positive way. An extra lift can be given to the last meeting, by members discussing at the previous meeting how they can bring along refreshments to turn the event into a party. Or, alternatively, the party can be separated from the regular series of meetings and held on a different occasion, leaving the last meeting for more 'serious' business to do with the purpose of the group. There will usually be a good deal to review and there may be benefit in people sharing plans, in the light of their experiences together.

The activity of reviewing can be carried out systematically, along the lines of the closure of the meeting described above. It may make sense to expand this activity, depending on the length of time the activity has been running, the intensity of the experience and so on. Sometimes group members get together to write newsletters, articles, or take photographs of such activities. It all depends on the degree of confidentiality and the extent of warm memories engendered by the experience. Some groups end rather suddenly, in the wake of unforeseeable difficulties. Others end on a high note with hugs and mutual thanks all round.

7

Empowering Community Groups and Organisations

Introduction

This chapter considers approaches to empowering work with and within community groups and organisations. How can the worker act so as to empower people in such settings? The first thing to recognise is that such work is essentially individually and group-based. Thus, many of the points made in earlier chapters about work with individuals and groups apply here. However, conditions in formal organisations are very different to community settings where the work may be with community associations or incipient self-help organisations. Second, empowering work is work *with* people. So, it involves approaches which engage with them, elicit their wishes, facilitate them formulating their own goals, address their needs, inequalities and/or disadvantages, and enable them to achieve their goals. Third, much of the material in this chapter on community empowerment is what community workers would recognise as community work.

A cautionary note

The framework for empowerment-in-practice outlined in Chapter 2 does not provide ready-made templates for the translation of empowering activity through the different levels, from individual to collective – organisationally or com-

116

munity-based – empowerment. The incidence of collective empowering activity in such settings is itself a contested area. To take one area as an example, the impulse towards collective social protest, which is often regarded as having reached its peak in the late 1960s in Western societies, appears to be in decline (see, for example, the conclusions of the study by Bagguley on political movements of unemployed people: Bagguley, 1991, p. 139). But in Britain during the early 1990s, the anti-poll-tax riots and protests against new motorway developments, blood sports and the exports of live animals to the rest of Europe, are a few examples which contradict such a conclusion. Again, as research into histories of protests by pupils (Adams, 1991) and prison riots (Adams, 1994) demonstrates, the incidence of protest may form a hidden history, not least when it involves oppressed groups or when it does not suit management to have incidents exposed to public or media scrutiny. Furthermore, such protest activity may be regarded as illegitimate by some people, and justified by others. So, the opportunities still remain for people to achieve self-realisation through empowering activity of various anti-oppressive kinds, whether or not involving overt protest.

General principles: anti-oppressive practice

Empowering social work through organisations and communities has the potential to combat multiple oppressions, which, as Thompson observes (Thompson, 1993, p. 122), may be interlocking and mutually reinforcing. The list of guidelines for white workers prepared by Twelvetrees from Ohri, Manning and Curno (1982) about working in non-racist ways could be adapted to apply to other aspects of oppression such as discrimination against people on the grounds of disability, age or sexuality:

1. Recognise that racism is a reality throughout British society.
2. Understand that racism is a white problem.
3. All of us need to find non-racist ways of working.

4. Recognise that you collude with racism.
5. Monitor whether the group or organisation in which you are involved is acting in a racist way
6. Your primary role is to challenge white racism (Supporting black self-help is secondary).
7. Do not confuse having relationships with black people with anti-racism.
8. Encourage other workers to work together to combat racism.
9. Familiarise yourself with issues of concern to the black community.

(Twelvetrees, 1991, p.150)

Process of the work

It is helpful to stand back behind the technicalities of working with people in organisations and communities and develop a checklist which encompasses different stages in the process of empowerment. Given our particular focus on self-help and user-led initiatives in this chapter, it may be helpful to draw on research from the field of self-help. Katz (1970) suggests that self-help organisations move through five stages in their life-histories: origins, informal organisation, the emergence of leadership, beginning of formal organisation, and the appointment of paid staff and professional workers. Let us take these in turn.

Stage 1: Origins

The starting point of the community-based or organisationally-based initiative may vary widely from setting to setting. It may be entirely autonomous, or it may arise from action by professionals. We begin by making some general observations on the latter circumstances.

Relationships between professionals and service users   The initiative may arise from professionals – let us assume they are social workers – developing a view about an area of need in a particular locality. Naturally, the extent to which the service can respond to the needs of the user depends partly on the availability of resources. Ideally, the service will be so responsive that service users actually write the specifications for the services they receive and participate in surveying the needs of their own user group, or become involved with workers in the process of determining how to work with their own user group. Methods of identifying the needs of service users and carers vary between, and sometimes within, authorities. The views of service users and carers, collectively and individually, may be sought in different ways, including involving them in consultative and planning meetings and surveying them using questionnaires and interviews. Collecting such information is by no means straightforward. At the outset, service users may be suspicious of survey techniques, especially if these involve strangers knocking at their doors. Older people, for example, who are warned often not to open their doors to strangers, may be inclined to refuse to co-operate with unscheduled callers. Moreover, some carers may not even identify themselves as such, having the view that they are simply friends, neighbours or relatives. Careful preparatory work may be necessary to gather information from service users and carers in such circumstances. Griffiths notes in the light of experience working with the carers' unit in Birmingham, that for consultation meetings with carers to be productive for all participants, they need to be composed of people from particular cultural backgrounds, rather than for mixed groups of carers. People's experiences of carers of racism and oppression also need to be tackled during the process of consultation. Also, consultation should be real rather than tokenistic, in the sense that it should fulfil people's expectations that their wishes will influence the kinds of services they receive (Griffiths, 1993, p.2). It is also essential that information about services and consultation processes reaches the people who are involved in them. Where necessary, information should be translated into different languages and jargon should be avoided in the drafting of leaflets. Care should be taken that information is not distorted in the translation process. Sometimes, information becomes drastically summarised in a process of redrafting and translating. It is important also to develop means of monitoring the extent to which the information has reached all the people who need access to it, whether directly or indirectly. It is essential to avoiding assuming that advocates for people who are disabled, older or mentally ill should be involved in these procedures, but not the people themselves.

Working with service users and carers in the community   Such work with users in specific groups highlights the need for the worker to have responsibility across the different agencies, and to have the right to be a member of the user group because of some shared experience with the users. For example, the effectiveness of the work may depend on the the person working with disabled people being disabled. But working in this way means that the worker needs the skills to be able to cope with the ambiguous role of being both a worker and a service user.

The experience of the 'Living Options in Practice' (1992) project suggests ways of identifying service users and carers and working with them. Such work is akin to community work. It uses local community resources and networks as locations for workers, service users and carers and other people to meet and exchange information. This emphasises how essential it is to involve local voluntary groups and organisations co-ordinating the voluntary sector, established self-help groups, carers' groups and user groups and individual service users and carers. All of these can act as sources of further information and contacts. Local purchasing and providing health and social care/social work agencies will need networking also. Those involved in the work will need to clarify what it involves as early as possible, and specify how it is to be monitored and evaluated.

Consultation with service users and carers Consultation meetings need careful planning, involving services users and carers in this process. Such a consultation needs to take place in a friendly, physically accessible location, which those attending will regard as 'neutral'. The meeting should be planned sufficiently far ahead to enable people to make arrangements with sitters and so on and to get release from work, to attend. The agency will need to take responsibility for determining the extent to which provision is possible to provide free or subsidised services for people who need child care and other services. Publicity will need to be used which is geared to the circumstances of the target group, taking due account of sensory disabilities and language differences, and producing duplicate notices and announcements on local radio and so on, in respective languages. The kinds of issues which may come up in the meeting will need anticipating by those organising it. Since one purpose of the meeting is for people to communicate their experiences and feelings as well as views, it will help if the organisers clearly how they will deal with situations where, for example, a participant criticises a particular worker, service user or carer. It will need to be clear in advance who should take the lead at the meeting and who will take part in giving introductions, talks, participate in discussions, summing up and concluding the meeting at the end. There will need to be arrangements for following up the meeting. These may need announcing at the meeting itself. Members should agree how the meeting is to be recorded and the arrangements to be made for evaluating its effectiveness.

The purpose of the Living Options in Practice project, written up for the King's Fund Centre, was to facilitate the setting up of comprehensive local services for adults with severe physical and sensory disabilities and to enable service users to participate significantly in assessing the needs for planning, implementing, monitoring and evaluating the services (Living Options in Practice, 1992). A worker appointed across the different provider agencies and purchaser authorities was engaged in this process. The following were the major areas of work entailed:

- making initial contact with disabled people
- arranging and carrying out consultation meetings and other events
- ensuring that information reached disabled people
- setting up and maintaining groups of service users
- ensuring joint working between professionals and service users
- organising appropriate training to enable people to make full use of the process
- securing ongoing funding for the user group on disabled people

(Living Options in Practice, 1992, *Project Paper No. 3, Achieving User Participation*, King's Fund Centre, London).

Stage 2: Informal organisation

Knight and Hayes give advice on the emergence and growth of self-help community groups (1981, ch. 6). New projects, they suggest, often need external help since community groups are in competition with other aspects of people's lives, people tend to adjust on an individualistic basis to problems and without a common objective, and deprivation itself may have an inhibiting effect on collective action. Additionally, political experience, knowledge and skill in running organisations and negotiating for resources are required (Knight and Hayes, 1981, p. 77). The argument that increasing state provision of services induces dependence, passivity and a decline in self-help and mutual aid, presents the potentially disastrous temptation to cut social provision in order to increase voluntary participation (Knight and Hayes, 1981, p. 78).

How is the group or organisation founded? It is paradoxical that founders of self-help groups and organisations so often have been professionals. In six out of ten organisations studied, Borman found that professionals played a key part in founding and early development (Borman, 1979, p. 21). Some self-help groups and organisations have been started by former members of other organisations. Thus, Synanon was founded by a former member of AA and this helps to explain the similarities in the purposes and operating principles of those two organisations. Often, those founding self-help organisations seek advice, either from someone involved in an existing activity or from sympathetic professionals, such as social workers, doctors, clergy, educationalists, workers in voluntary agencies and others.

It is common for participants in self-help activities at the birth of the group or organisation to experience anxiety or panic about the future of the self-help initiative itself (Lindenfield and Adams, 1984, p. 20). This is in addition to any anxieties experienced in connection with the problem or issues for which self-help is sought. In part, this is the reason why in the very early stages many people give up and many young self-help initiatives perish.

At the community level, organisational factors may weigh heavily in the founding days of an empowering initiative. Three factors identified in respect of effective partnership in social services can be applied here. First, there are questions of ideology reflected in the attitude of the local authority agencies towards involvement with the voluntary sector; second, there is the availability of resources from sources such as local authority departments and central government; third, there is the degree of priority given by the local authority to the area or client group served by the voluntary body (Jones, 1981, pp. 6–7).

Work with organisations needs to be carried out with an awareness of their nature and function. Large formal organisations such as social work and social services departments are likely to be relatively formal and bureaucratic, in contrast with a community association, which may vary in size, but is likely in reality to be run by a handful of volunteers who take most of the decisions and do much of the work. A feature shared by larger, more complex organisations, whether in the statutory, voluntary or private sectors, is that they are not geared particularly to empowering individuals. Workers, like other members, may even experience them as oppressive.

Reducing inequalities Research supported by the Social Services Inspectorate demonstrates the need to rectify gender imbalances in the personal social services, exemplified by the fact that whereas women are the main users and providers of services, they play only a marginal part in the management of social services. Empowerment is viewed by the SSI as a key strategy by which to address this alarming situation (SSI, 1991, p. 55). What if the imbalances are present in the self-help or user-led organisation? How far should the professional intervene and how far should a distance be maintained from the way the organisation is run?

Cumulative or contained empowerment Efforts to develop an empowering culture in an organisation or community setting may be successful, in which case the ripples from the original initiative will spread outwards, as more and more people are empowered. On the other hand, an initiative may lead to the formation of a clique of converts to the new approach and, because other people either are apathetic or hostile towards the initiative, organisational or community development may be minimal.

Stage 3: Emergence of leadership

What sort of leadership emerges? In the early days, it is not only the new member but also the group itself which is vulnerable. Despite the fact that in the early stages members may be very enthusiastic, this enthusiasm can evaporate very quickly if certain basic requirements are not met. The bread-and-butter of organising and leading meetings, for instance, is no less crucial because its importance is obvious. What often distinguishes many self-help initiatives from professional ones is the way in self-help the task of leadership is shared by several people. It is commonly said that effective groups are democratically led. But in self-help the knowledge and skills which underpin this leadership need to be demonstrated by a sufficient number of participants in order to sustain a broad consensus about group goals, a good level of communication and a degree of participation which gives all those involved an appropriate stake in what is going on (Lindenfield and Adams, 1984, p. 22).

Knight and Hayes observe, in the light of studying thirty community self-help groups, that the very characteristics of strong leadership by articulate individuals which help to establish them, are likely to inhibit their subsequent development (Knight and Hayes, 1981, p. 88). The maintenance of activities which involve local people depends subsequently on reducing the emphasis on bureaucratic activity and formal meetings, reducing dependence on middle-class and/or professional leadership and developing social events alongside the other purposes of the group or activities.

On the contrary, the problem may be addressed by empowering what Knight and Hayes (1981, p. 50) term 'reticulists'. They define reticulists, as young, middle-class, articulate and socially and politically committed. Whilst they may succeed in initiating groups, this may perpetuate the elitist tendency for such people to retain leadership of activities which ideally might have been owned and run by poor and deprived people (Knight and Hayes, 1981, p. 79).

Stage 4: Beginning of formal organisation

Will a formal self-help organisation emerge? Unlike many organisations, self-help initiatives do not invariably pass beyond the first stage of their founding to a more formal organisational stage. The initial founders do not automatically hand over to professional administrators. In this respect, Borman's study (1979) stands in sharp contrast with the earlier work of Katz. None of the ten groups Borman studied developed comparably with Katz's groups. Nevertheless, Borman reports (Borman, 1979, p. 41) that Katz later found (Katz and Bender, 1976, p. 122) that the growth of formal organisation and professionals were not universal features of self-help groups.

Perhaps the reason for this seemingly obstinate refusal of self-help groups to behave like emergent formal organisations is the simple fact that they differ from them in major ways. Not least, autonomous self-help initiatives in particular differ in that they are founded by lay members and many later retain their local, small-scale character. Obviously, exceptions such as AA are significant, if only because they stand out as exceptions to the great mass of small initiatives which live and die at a very local level. At a bureaucratic extreme perhaps, Mended Hearts, a medical self-help organisation, has grown to mimic the kind of organisation that self-help often sets out to shun. Bond comments that:

> as self-help groups become large organisations, it is more difficult for new individuals to become personally involved in the group's core activities. The large formal meetings lead most participants to view themselves as an audience. For members who are not involved in a help-giving capacity (that is, non-visitors), perceived benefits of group membership are minimal, and their peripheral involvement in the organisation is underscored. (Bond *et al.*, 1979, p. 59)

At a more modest level, it is easy to see how groups planning more than one meeting at a time move towards a division of the labour which this involves, from chairing and administering, to taking notes of decisions, writing letters and acting as treasurer or caterer. Not many groups survive without at least finding reliable ways of distributing these tasks and ensuring they are carried out responsibly.

How will self-help develop into helping others? Another way in which a self-help group may develop is through the original group changing its focus from an inward-directed view. This may be achieved by inviting outsiders, such as speakers or students, to contribute to meetings (Lindenfield and Adams, 1984, p. 95). Clearly the presence of an outsider changes the character of a group and may have a dramatic impact, turning the participants towards some new activity or in an unexpected direction.

A group or organisation may reach the stage where members become involved in educational events as part of their role in the group, although members of less well-established groups may be less likely to do this. They may need encouragement from others. Courses and conferences may happen, to which a group can send representatives. Such events often will welcome non-professionals and some will reduce fees for members of self-help groups. A grant may be obtained for attendance at a training course. The local Council for Voluntary Service (CVS) or Adult Education Centre may make provision for people to be sponsored on such a course. Topics on such courses may include coping with depression, issues of race and gender, raising children alone, unemployment and finding work, looking after elderly people, voluntary action and, last but not least, running self-help activities.

Involvement in local community or wider issues comes more easily to some groups than to others. Some groups may be more used to taking up issues than others, for instance by becoming involved in activities which raise community awareness, through some form of information gathering locally or an educational campaign concerning a health issue. As time passes, some groups or organisations develop outside activities to the point where their resources begin to stimulate the growth of other helping activities in the community., While some groups, notably consciousness-raising groups, have this more or less built into their aims, others may move towards it slowly and with difficulty. Those involved may need the encouragement of a ready-provided rationale.

Three justifications can be given. First, those who have met to help themselves and each other have demonstrated already their commitment and motivation and may have reached the point where they would stimulated by, and help others through, a wider focus for their efforts. Second, groups need to avoid becoming insular and should benefit from keeping in touch with local developments. Third, groups may find it fruitful to encourage and support other people who are interested in self-help but have not yet taken the plunge (Lindenfield and Adams, 1984, p. 94). But the growth of formal organisation is not predicated upon outside activities. They are used here as an example of typical developments which would produce pressure towards it.

Clearly, another positive direction in which self-helpers may move is towards more overt community work. Alan Twelvetrees (1982) and Paul Henderson (Henderson and Thomas, 1980, pp. 148–86) have commented on the stages involved in the process of community work. Twelvetrees identifies nine stages in work with community groups, paraphrased below:

1. Contacting people and analysing needs
2. Bringing people together, helping them to identify needs and developing the will to meet those needs
3. Helping people understand what will need doing for needs to be met
4. Adopting objectives
5. Creating a suitable organisation to this end
6. Helping them to form a plan of action, breaking down broad goals into smaller objectives and tasks
7. Helping them allocate and carry out the consequent tasks
8. Helping them to feed back and evaluate results of the action and adopt fresh objectives in the light of this
9. Enabling them to take on the repetition of stages 3 to 8, whereupon the worker withdraws to a servicing role.

(Twelvetrees, 1991, pp. 35–6)

Stage 5: Appointment of paid staff and professional workers

Can paid or professional staff be employed by self-helpers? Although it is difficult to generalise about its nature and timing, there does seem to be a point where increasing outward-directedness of some self-help groups and organisations pushes participants towards establishing a formal organisation with all that implies. This may sound as though it contradicts the principles of self-help, but it is easy to see how self-helpers may move towards it.

Some striking examples of groups and networks exist, such as the 'anonymous' organisations referred to in Chapter 5, many of which employ paid staff. However, as in any organisation, the fact that an organisation may be run by users does not mean that it will necessarily empower its own paid staff. This is an aspect of moving towards a formal organisation which will generate particular contradictions, including whether or not the professional worker has a right, or a role, to intervene.

We move now to consider examples which illustrate many of the aspects covered above. Both of these were originally written in the late 1980s, but the issues they point to are still relevant.

Example 1: The Humberside Project

An example of an attempt to empower people is provided by the Humberside Project, a partnership between Save the Children Fund and Humberside Social Services Department. This aimed to create a series of self-help neighbourhood settings leading to shared management of resources devoted to work with parents and children. Initially, the emphasis was on the under-fives and the first two work bases included a council house and an existing playgroup on two housing estates in Grimsby. Project staff aimed throughout to encourage parents to take a lead in making decisions about the kinds of activities and provision for young children they would like in the neighbourhood. Since December 1986 when project workers started, parents became involved in running drop-in facilities for parents and toddlers and play- groups elsewhere in the estates, as well as groups exclusively for mothers.

The concept of user involvement in management was central to the Humberside Project. It was nurtured through three years of planning before implementation, during which staff in Save the Children Fund (SCF) and Humberside Social Services worked through issues concerning partnership. Eventually it was agreed that during the developmental period the project would be run by SCF, serviced by their regional resources and development worker, other staff salaries and expenses being met by social services in anticipation of the eventual handover of the entire project to the social services department, some five years after its commencement.

Less than a year after the commencement of work at the first workbase, the workers and parents were agreed that progress had been made towards the handover of management of the project to local users, as originally envisaged by the agencies. An evaluation of this project carried out by the writer produced the following illustration of the empowerment process, from the perception of a neighbourhood team manager, responsible for the rnage of social services in one of the estates served by the project:

> You obviously want a small unit of the kind we envisaged: a continual throughput, people come, they make contact, they grow, they develop, they get confidence, they move out and start to do likewise elsewhere. . . . We are significantly down the road towards local management, local people using the project. I had anticipated a build-up of local people, wanting to be involved in decision-making. In fact the pressure from them is quite strong, wanting to be involved in things . . . The ripples are going outward now, wider, to more organisations now, and I hope going out to a higher range as well, so that it's more an assumed attitude people have towards their children and their needs rather than just a build-up of social facilities or a collection of activities. It's much more comprehensive than that . . . the local authority almost becomes a local financial

source only and people locally feel themselves sufficiently confident in handling their own affairs to run something which operates reasonably cheaply and provides a service which keys together everything that's going on in the neighbourhood.

Integral self-help involves the paradox that sponsoring social work agencies resource and professionally support the move towards self-help by consumers of their services. The manager quoted above describes this:

> You do have to keep some kind of hand on the tiller, you do have to think about it as an organisation and give it the kind of support and development help that it needs from time to time. But I see it ultimately very much as an enabling function community work-wise, which sustains the growth and development of something which is very much about empowering local people.

Associated with the empowerment process, it is typical to encounter a variety of resources being brought to bear, some of which lie outside the range of social work provision. Thus the social worker acts as the negotiator who initiates the activity and then builds up a multi-disciplinary, multi-professional approach. Thus in the Humberside Project, from the initial overtures made to parents a number of training courses developed, in aspects of play and parenting. At a later stage, parents undertook courses together, arranged on-site, which led to a number becoming registered as play leaders. From that point, they were able to share with project workers, as volunteers and as paid workers themselves, some of the basic tasks of supervising play activities and ensure that there was time and resources to carry out further development work in the community.

Example 2: Asian Resource Centre

A well-established example of a self-help organisation functioning largely autonomously from social services agencies was the Asian Resource Centre (ARC) in Birmingham, which came about through a grassroots initiative by people involved in a multi-cultural centre called Action Centre. Workers involved at that time noted the need for a centre specifically designed to meet the needs of Asian people. The ARC was located in a street of shops in Handsworth and acted as a community centre for the Asian community:

> in the relevant languages with a deep understanding of the religious and cultural aspirations of the people it serves. The services are provided through advice work at the Centre, running appropriate projects like the Asian Elders, Women's Welfare Rights, Housing Welfare etc., and by providing resources and practical help in such areas as immigration, nationality and anti-sexism. The Centre produces leaflets, pamphlets in Asian languages and acts as a pressure group to statutory services. It provides educational and training facilities for the local community, voluntary and statutory agencies. The Centre is staffed by Asian workers and managed by elected representatives of the Asian community. (Asian Resource Centre, 1987)

The aims of the ARC were stated as follows: first, 'to identify and analyse the cultural and the social system placed upon particularly disadvantaged sections of the Asian community within the neighbourhood and elsewhere, and also identify its general and specific needs'; second, 'to initiate, participate and assist in projects designed to protect their civil and human rights, to encourage freedom of cultural expression and encourage all Asians to reassert their cultural identity, self confidence and pride' (Birmingham Asian Resource Centre, 1987).

The management committee of the ACR comprised eighteen people, including ten members elected by open vote at the Annual General Meeting, five who were co-opted for their particular skills and two councillors who represented the Local Authority. Its seven full-time workers were funded by the Inner City Partnership Programme, the Housing Authority, the Social Service Department, Cadbury Trust and other donations and funds. An effort was made to maintain a balanced staff team, reflecting Bengali, Pakistani and Punjab (Indian) interests, in its broad range of community-oriented activities.

The ACR exemplified the autonomous sector of self-help, in that it came into being as a result of the awareness of groups in the community that their needs were not being met by professionals and who were motivated to generate a self-help initiative to that end.

Commentary

Several themes emerge from such examples, which have more general relevance to the empowerment endeavours of social workers:

The paradox of power The concept of empowerment through integral self-help implies the paradox that professionals exercise power in their commitment to providing the initial resources; they suggest directions in which the activities move, but at the same time try to stand back and let the self-helpers put their own definition on what happens.

Whose definition of the goals of empowerment do we accept? The fact that empowerment is fashionable as a goal of workers involved in developing self-help heightens a dilemma for practice: whether to proceed on the basis of the view of the social worker or of the potential self-helpers. It is common to find parents involved in the early stages of such initiatives as the Humberside Project expressing hesitance about, or even refusing to consider, taking on responsibility for managing the project. Should the workers proceed with goals they themselves have determined, or accept from the outset a view of the activity as defined by the parents themselves? This is a difficult question, to which there is no easy answer. In many ways, the most realistic approach is to maintain open dialogue between social workers and self-helpers about such issues from the earliest days. There is some evidence that as the latter develop in confidence and competence, their ambitions to take on a more participative role in the activity also grow.

Personal growth and professional competence   It is important to develop a view of empowerment through self-help which re-cognises these two are linked themes for both social workers and self-helpers, rather than as separated by the roles of pro-fessional and user. Ideally, empowerment as a process should embrace all parties to social work: workers, clients, organisa-tions, self-helpers, and all networks.

An open-ended process rather than a single-outcome activity   The most noticeable feature of this approach to self-help is the lack of one single milestone which could be said to mark the outcome of the project. Instead, typically activities are perceived as processes, in which the personal and profes-sional aspects referred to above develop in an open-ended way. One of the striking features of such processes is the way professionals and self-helpers exchange roles and responsi-bilities as the project moves on. Thus, in the Humberside Pro-ject, quite quickly one of the parents, a mother who had never taken this kind of task before, used the support of the project to start two parent and toddler groups. She com-mented that: 'Instead of being just a housewife I am begin-ning to feel important especially when the mums at the group come to me for help and advice. I feel that I am a seed from the project that has grown and is now planting her own seeds.'

A replicable approach   In answer to queries about whether such a project is central to the social work task, two comments are necessary: first, it is increasingly common to find health, edu-cation, social work and voluntary agencies combining with parents in self-help groups, to develop better facilities for par-ents and children under five; second, this example provides a model which is easily transferable to other client groups in different geographical locations.

Towards community education   In setting out the agenda of empowerment in this section, partly in terms of the goal of shifting from integral to autonomous self-help, we need to make explicit the continuum which exists between what social workers engage in and the work of the community educators. In the Humberside Project, one of the most exciting developments has been the establishing by the project workers of a new series of basic course in family and neighbourhood work, in conjunction with local adult educational staff in Grimsby. Undoubtedly, there is much scope for social workers to work across professional boundaries with educational providers and improve both access and ladders of opportunity and qualification in many sectors of learning. Community education is not just new classes in the community. It should be voluntarily negotiated, community-derived learning, which non-professionals can initiate as a means of reducing social inequalities, promoting change and empowering people.

8

Empowering Evaluation

Introduction

Evaluation is central to social work. There are two major justifications for evaluation: as a contribution to reflective practice and as a means of achieving systematic feedback on the quality of practice. This chapter examines the impact of the paradigm of empowerment on the task of evaluation. It provides clarification on different approaches which may be adopted and some guidelines on how to carry out evaluation in an empowering way. It illustrates how empowerment-in-practice may achieved by evaluating through experiment-in-practice, with the evaluator as experient and co-producer, as referred to in the framework in Chapter 2 (Figure 2.1).

Avoiding shortcomings of much evaluation

A common feature of evaluation of practice is the lack of attention given to thinking through the way it is carried out, before engaging in it. Sometimes, evaluation is invested with too much significance, especially when managers try to impose it as a tool to brush up the quality of practice. Thorpe notes that the pressure for quality, in the education sector and in private enterprise, may lead to evaluation being redesignated as quality assurance (Thorpe, 1993, p. xv). Evaluation may be imposed on practitioners and/or service users from line managers, or from outside the work setting. Thus, they may receive a request, or an instruction, to co-operate with a visiting interviewer and may have little or no control over the design, execution, analysis, or subsequent use of the data being collected about their practice. If this approach leaves practitioners feeling disempowered, it is easy to imagine how service users feel when they are on the receiving end of this approach to data collection. Frequently also, evaluation is remembered *after* the action has begun, or even worse, at the end, when attempts may be made rather belatedly to 'build in some research into what we're doing' rather than developing the evaluation from the planning stage of the social work activity. Although *post hoc*, or 'after the event' evaluation of practice can be undertaken, it is much more difficult to carry out effectively. Both of these features of evaluative research are diametrically opposed to the standpoint of this chapter, since empowering evaluation *must* involve the major stakeholders, *including service users*, from its earliest stage.

Kuhn comments that the process of learning a theory depends on the study of its applications (Kuhn, 1970, pp. 47). As Chapter 2 notes, the development of the paradigm of empowerment and the working out of its application to the many different areas of social work, are processes which are occurring simultaneously.

In this light, we identify four features of empowering evaluation:

- The evaluation is likely to involve the participants, whether workers, service users, carers, or all of these, as co-producers and/or as experiencers, in managing and carrying it out themselves, as self-managed research.
- Any attempt to carry out an evaluation of practice should endeavour to collaborate with, and thus empower, the service user – the major stakeholder most vulnerable to exclusion from key aspects of the process. This is part of what Freire means by the dialogic activity, referred to in Chapter 4.

- The most productive research methodology is likely to be experiment-in-practice or action-based, rather than following traditional experimental method.
- In all probability where practitioners and/or service users are doing the evaluation themselves without relief from other responsibilities, a case study, or critical appraisal, of the action will be more useful than quantitative, statistically based, evaluation.

Experiment-in-practice rather than traditional experimental method

The commitment to using experiment-in-practice as a means of carrying out empowering evaluation arises from Schon's view of the practitioner as experimenting through the process of reflective action (Schon, 1991, pp. 141–53). Schon maintains that reflection in action must involve experiment, through the rigor of evaluating the entire process of reflecting on examples of action and reframing them. This is likely to involve problem-setting. Practitioners thereby address a number of questions: 'whether they can solve the problem they have set; whether thay value what they get when they solve it (or what they can make of what they get); whether they achieve in the situation a coherence of artifact and idea, a congruence with their fundamental theories and values; whether they can keep inquiry moving' (Schon, 1991, p. 141). This process differs fundamentally from traditional approaches to experiment, involving hypothesis testing or controlled experiment. Schon points out that reflection-in-action violates the basic conditions of controlled experiments requiring that the researcher maintain distance from the behaviour observed, but is no less rigorous, since the practitioner continually tests, modifies and retests theories and hypotheses embedded in the action, reframing as necessary, in affirmation of the hypothesis or to explore further.

Clarifying the task

By adopting the term 'critical appraisal' (see Key, Hudson and Armstrong, 1976, pp. 44–6 for a fine description of the use of this term) in this chapter, we are proposing a realistic approach to evaluation, rather than downgrading its essential contribution to practice and, what is often overlooked, the development of practice theory, or theory through practice. By this means, evaluation has the potential to benefit service users as well as to cultivate criticality in reflective practitioners. The term 'appraisal' describes the attempt to feed back to people answers to questions they pose about what they are doing, how they are doing it and how 'well' they are doing it. On the whole, the sort of appraisal which those involved in empowerment will encounter is concerned with the present or the immediate past rather than with the future. That is, the most common question to which an answer will be sought by means of appraisal is: 'how have we been doing in this activity?' But the equally important sequel should be 'what does this mean?' and then, 'so what!' or 'what do we do now?'

We have to start by asking what the rationale is for appraising a particular empowering activity. Is it absolutely essential for some purpose, desirable, or merely contemplated out of interest?

Appraisal is not simply a major means of ensuring a rational process of decision-making concerning the future of a project or activity. Very rarely, as Key *et al.* (1976, p. 31) notes, is appraisal actually given this degree of prominence by policy-makers or managers. All too rarely are resources made available for practitioners to evaluate their activities. In the field of empowerment, there is a singular dearth of research. There is a noticeable lack of evaluative studies of self-help groups, for example. It was noted in the mid-1970s that 'to date, not a single adequate study of the effectiveness of self-help groups exists' (Lieberman and Borman, 1976, p. 459). The fact that in Britain this is still largely true should not deter the practitioner at this stage. It is even more important for the results of any systematic critical reflection on practice to be presented as one among many sources of information on which all of us – private individuals, service users, professionals and agency managers – may draw when we make our decisions. The actual rationale for evaluating an empowering activity may be different from the justification presented in public. But for all that, it is still crucial for the appraisal to be carried out as well as possible.

Appraisal as an empowering tool

A more positive way to view the process and the outcome of appraisal of an empowering activity is that, used sensitively and constructively, it can be a means of empowering both service users and social workers. It should not be used so as to perpetuate the oppression of those in whose interests it is allegedly carried out! Cunningham (1994, pp. 164–7) provides a helpful list of principles which guide what he calls interactive holistic research. It is collaborative, dialogic, experiential, action based and contextualising. *Collaborative* refers to the joint pursuit of the appraisal by a group of people. *Dialogic* is the term used to describe the interaction between two people which is used as the basis for collecting the data. *Experiential* refers to the focus on the direct experience of the person and/or the worker. It can be personal, where the researcher and the subject are the same person, or involve the response to the experience being shared with other people. *Action based* refers to the widely used concept of action research, keeping the active doing as the central focus of the process. *Contextualising* refers to the process of feeding off and into the context in which the action takes place.

We can construct a checklist of questions to help clarify before proceeding:

For whom are we doing it?

All sorts of people may be receivers of the appraisal. It may be carried out for professionals, for service users, for agency funders or managers, for a mixture of these or for other people altogether such as journalists, students or academics doing independent research.

Sources of sponsorship The sources of sponsorship or commissioning will affect the nature of the audience for which any report is eventually written (see the section on 'producing and using the appraisal' below). It also affects how quickly they expect results. Generally speaking, academics expect results far less quickly than practitioners, so it is as well for the accountability of the evaluator as evaluator to be specified clearly at the outset, with the agreement of all stakeholders in the appraisal.

Who controls the appraisal?

We can exemplify the question of control by contrasting the traditional situation, where the researcher has total control and no one else affects the appraisal, with the interactive situation. This is much more likely to empower other people, since the researcher and the service users collaborate at every stage in the process of addressing all of the questions laid out in this chapter. On the whole, the more consultative the appraisal, the more time-consuming the process of continually meeting to carry it out collaboratively, but the more rewarding for all parties the sense of joint ownership of the eventual results (Patton, 1982, pp. 55–98).

What kind of appraisal is sought?

As we saw above, clarifying who are the sponsors and the audience helps to clarify the kind of research envisaged. Between them, they are likely to be interested in questions generated here for the sake of illustration, from within one or more of the following categories selected from those listed by Patton (1982, p. 44):

Front-end analysis

* Is there evidence in advance to justify starting an empowering activity?
* Are local conditions such that empowering activity is feasible?
* Are there enough potential service users in this field in this locality?

Formative appraisal

* What activities are going on?
* What is the story of empowerment in action, in this particular setting?
* What needs to be done in order to improve this programme of empowerment?

Impact or summative evaluation

* What effects and outcomes has this empowering activity had
* What is its basic worth?

The distinction between hard-line and soft-line approaches (Key *et al.*, 1976, pp. 10–11) is useful. The former rely more on the notions of scientific evaluation we might encounter in the world of business or the natural sciences while the latter are more concerned with impressionistic, subjective or experience-based findings.

A common approach: critical appraisal by case study

This is the term we use to cover both formative and summative studies of empowering activities in the list above. It may often involve a case-study approach. The preference for this is based partly on grounds of the time and other resource constraints which are likely to rule out more full-blooded approaches to evaluation. But in addition, there is a real danger that evaluations of this kind could intimidate service users, put them into a relatively passive and powerless situation or in other words disempower them.

A case study involves the following:

1. It is flexible, in that research questions, goals, hypotheses can be altered as the study proceeds.
2. It generally involves the researcher in some kind of relatively unstructured observation.
3. It invariably necessitates the researcher being reflexive, that is using her or his own reactions to a situation as a source of data, further reflection and evaluative activity.
4. It is geared to understanding the process of the activity rather than simply pronouncing after it has finished, on the outcomes.

The process of carrying out a case study necessitates:

1. getting access to the evidence: i.e., being patient while people get familiar enough to begin to share confidences; being around often enough and/or long enough to get a feel of what is going on
2. looking for typical, as well as rare or unusual cases, situations, incidents, processes; trying to compare, contrast and understand these
3. maintaining a sense of theoretical issues raised by the research
4. keeping in touch with the sources of evidence throughout
5. remaining open to fresh ideas and interpretations.

What is being appraised?

Is the subject of appraisal a short-lived activity which took place some weeks or months ago, on which retrospective information is sought? Is it current, or planned at some time in the near future? Is it a newly established or a well-established meeting, with a single, local intermittent base or a national network of federated groups?

These questions about the character, scope and scale of the appraisal greatly affect the nature of the research devised.

Preparing for the appraisal

In general, the approach to appraisal should be sufficiently flexible to capture the unexpected and yet sufficiently specific to enable reasonably precise, objective and valid judgements to be made.

What sources of information are sought?

Will a single individual or group activity be used as a source, or a sample of these? Will one kind of source be sought, or a variety of sources? The choice here is between aiming at depth of cover from one kind of source, or trying to achieve corroboration of the evidence from more than one direction, by using different sources. The criticality of the evaluation depends on its reference to the context as well as to the key participants, including service users.

Appraisal may also be considered from a vantage point *outside the activity*. For instance, the extinction of the original problem or issue which led to its initiation may in theory be marked by the activity itself coming to an end. So, far from determining the effectiveness of empowerment in terms of the number of new activities which come into existence, or the length of time they have been in existence, it may be more relevant to monitor the number of activities which terminate.

But this itself is problematic, since activities may finish because participants become frustrated or bored, through ineffectiveness or the intransigence of problems of one or more participants.

How much information should we collect?

Clearly, the argument about whether collecting data from surveys of larger numbers of people is preferable to small-scale work, can be settled in practical terms by the constraints on time which prevent many appraisals becoming large-scale. But there is a positive argument also for small numbers or even single case studies. Patton puts the point forcibly:

> It is worth remembering that some of the major breakthroughs in knowledge have come from studies with small sample sizes. Freud's work was based on a few clinical cases. Piaget significantly changed educational thinking about how children learn with an in-depth study of two children – his own. (Patton, 1982, p. 219)

We may criticise Patton's choice of illustrations, but the case for very small-scale case studies is still valid, based on the high pay-off which can be achieved in terms of scope of information and qualitative depth.

Three pieces of advice need to be borne in mind:

- Pose one, or a small number, of key questions which the appraisal will address and collect only such informations as will contribute to answering these.
- Don't collect too much data. It will only clutter up your filing cabinet and eventually, long after you have failed to use it, find its way into the rubbish basket.
- Keep in mind the need to write a short, concise report and collect evidence to this end, and not for the sake of collecting it.

What evidence will be collected?

The great variety of ways of gathering evidence – from surveys, questionnaries and interviews of a more or less structured kind, to direct observation of activities – affects the kinds of evidence collected. Johnston Birchall convincingly argues that case histories of co-operative practice in the field of housing – very similar in character to many self-help or user-led activities – may be evaluated in terms of six key variables (Birchall, 1988, pp. 162–88). Adapting these to the empowerment field produces the following useful list:

1. *Participation*: including 'true believers' who willingly participate, 'freeloaders' who like to benefit without sharing the costs of participating, 'sceptical conformers' who conform without participating actively, 'holdouts' who refuse to conform but remain in the activity and 'escapees' who would leave if given half a chance
2. *Extensity:* the size of the activity and its geographical concentration
3. *Duration:* the time the activity has existed
4. *Adequacy:* the ability of participants to reach the common goals
5. *Intensity:* the depth of commitment participants have to each other
6. *Purity:* the commitment of participants to the principles of the activity.

A direct indication of the value of the activity to people can be obtained simply by asking them about the experience. From the participant's point of view, the success of empowerment may be seen in terms of whether she or he feels better or happier, or more in control of everyday life, whether esteem has increased, whether personal relationships have improved and whether the activity has been enjoyable. Undoubtedly, such information is hard to validate on an objective basis, independently of the judgements of participants themselves. But it remains part of a widespread movement which treats the way participants define their situation as the paramount source of data on effectiveness of an activity.

Another approach is to examine the quality of life of participants, in such major areas as work, leisure and unemployment, relationships and family experiences. A further aspect of the focus on the experience of participants is to compare the perceptions of people who seek the activity being studied and those who do not.

In these circumstances, the key question is what motivates some people to take part, whether the factors concerned reflect differences in the circumstances of individuals in social or in psychological terms.

Problems of information gathering

There may be a conflict at the outset between the values of the researcher and those of people involved in activities. At the very least this may lead to people involved in such activities being unwilling to co-operate in research. They may refuse to talk about themselves or to provide written information. They may refuse to allow the researcher access to their activities, to gather any kind of direct evidence to enable corroboration with documentary data. This is particularly likely in the case of activities independent of professionals. Penny Webb's attempt to monitor a scheme designed to stimulate the setting-up of self-help groups encountered problems of this kind, some people being unwilling to fill in questionnaires and others being unable to cope with them (Webb, 1982, p. 125). Lieberman and Borman (1976, p. 461) found that groups were resistant to outsiders intruding on their activities.

The values of empowering activities may conflict with the more traditional helping activities with which researchers may wish to compare them. Thus, what many other professionals may see as the very idiosyncratic values of some empowering activities may further inhibit the straightforward appraisal of their effectiveness. It has been said that unlike psychotherapy, which emphasises honesty and self-understanding, self-help groups may encourage denial and the construction of mythologies (Lieberman and Borman, 1976, p. 229). In other words, just as some would argue that the doctor has an interest in writing a prescription in a form which mystifies the lay person and preserves professional, power and mystique, so it may be argued that the alternative practitioner of empowerment may develop a similar defence, albeit from a very different perspective.

Is the evaluator more interested in the *process* or in the *outcome* of the empowering activity? Who else has questions to ask? What other stakeholders have an interest, actually or potentially, in the appraisal of the activity? Whose questions have the prior claim? These are questions which concern the political and ethical dimensions of the activity. Generally speaking, there are no clear, easy or unchanging answers to them.

There are also questions of focus, which bear on the evaluative approach adopted. For instance, whereas approaches which emphasise the process bring out aspects such as the quality of the experience, those which focus on outcomes of empowerment tend to highlight its impact on participants and comparisons with the impact of other kinds of activity. These issues are affected by the vantage point from which the appraisal is carried out whether inside the activity, outside it, or a mixture of both. The following are relevant questions to consider in this connection:

Is the person doing the appraisal as part of the action, or a total outsider? Is she or he an experienced researcher, or a novice? Is she or he a professional, or a lay person going it alone, or a worker, or a student receiving regular relevant supervision and support? Has this person an interest to declare? That is, what is the motivation for the appraisal: personal interest, utility to an outside professional or agency, benefit to the service users or another external purpose such as contribution to research based elsewhere?

Permutations of the situation of the evaluator may be devised from three basic options: an external specialist evaluator not employed by the service users or the relevant professional agency, an internal specialist evaluator employed directly by the agency and/or service users, or service users and/or involved social workers themselves.

Key (*et al.*, 1976, pp. 25–7) summarises the issues raised by the choice of evaluator. On the whole, the more 'inside' a person is, the more acceptable to peers, the cheaper the appraisal and the closer to the intimacies of what is happening when it comes to presenting a fearlessly critical and objective account. On the other hand, the further 'outside' the evaluator stands, the more the claim of objective distance will have to be balanced against the time spent getting close to the complex heart of things. Objectivity also may be claimed, but no more achieved, by the outsider than by the insider. All researchers, whether they acknowledge it or not, occupy a value stance which to an extent permeates the way they plan, carry out and interpret their research.

Finally, Patton (1982, p. 223) notes that the whole debate should not be presented, as it often is, in terms of alternatives, since in practice many effective appraisals have been carried out by combinations of insiders and outsiders working together.

Process studies

The study of action processes often is more feasible and productive than looking for outcomes, especially in relatively long-term or open-ended groups, projects or schemes. In many ways, process studies are incompatible with evaluative research since they tend to concentrate on the life history of a group, activity, scheme, project or organisation and/or the nature of the experience of involvement from the standpoint of participants. To this extent they may be descriptive and involve qualitative methods of data collection, for instance, with particular regard to the way members experience being in a group. It is often said that experience expresses its own inherent validity in the uniqueness of its subjective quality. Advocates of this view may argue the superiority of process-based research over externally-based appraisal of outcomes.

Yet it is important to recognise that this polarisation between process and outcome studies is somewhat artificial. It is not necessary for intuitive reflection on group processes to obliterate appraisal of group outcomes. The two may be regarded as complementary. In the study of twenty various self-help groups, Levy found that they were dealing not only with their members' problems but also with their most fundamental human needs, such as 'for empathic understanding, for enhanced self-esteem, for meaning, and for an opportunity to express their feelings and share their experiences with another' (Levy, 1979, p. 217). He suggests this may explain why most members would expect to stay indefinitely in their groups.

Studying involvement In one respect, process studies contribute invaluable insights to evaluative research. The context in which the effectiveness of a self-help group is evaluated tends to be as transient as the lives of many groups themselves. Clearly, self-help activities are not often as long-lived as organisations and institutions such as social work teams, hospitals or community care providers.

Having said that, members of some self-help and user-led initiatives are likely to feel justifiably proud, not so much of the speed with which they gained control of their problems, but of the number of years they have been members of a group or organisation. Membership is too unspecific a term to apply to the multitude of levels of attendance, involvement and intensity which is possible in a self-help programme. One member may attend every meeting for years but remain relatively invisible in the group, while another attends occasionally but is always noticeable. The sporadic attendance of a third over a long period may correspond with intermittent stresses in everyday life. Again, it is worth considering the kind of organisation which involves a postal network. How does one set out to assess outcomes in such circumstances?

Studying membership succession A further complication arises when one considers that many groups and organisations attract successions of members in view of their open-ended character. The term 'serial reciprocity' has been used (Richardson and Goodman, 1983, p. 96) to describe the pattern of involvement by means of which members feed back into groups some form of support after they themselves have been helped. This seems to be one of the most effective ways in which members can contribute to group life. We can anticipate also that over a period, different members will be at different stages in the process. However, patterns of participation differ according to the nature of the focus which draws people together. It has been observed that those caring for relatives of people with learning disabilities tend to remain long-term members of self-help groups, in contrast with the generally brief membership of widows and single parents (Richardson and Goodman, 1983, p. 97).

In this connection, it helps if sufficient experienced members are present in an open-ended group to give stability and continuity, without it becoming so top heavy that the new, potential members are discouraged from joining. It may be helpful also for members to feel that they are all at the same stage of discussing and coming to terms with their problems (Richardson and Goodman, 1983, p. 98) and this may even militate against open-ended groups.

So before and after measurement or testing, even if service users allowed it, would not necessarily illuminate the quality of the experience of empowerment. Neither would it identify events in the lives of group members, such as accidents, traumas or one-off incidents.

Outcome studies

Appraisal may take a number of forms: individual outcomes, comparative outcomes, impact on the activity or its context. It is possible to view the outcome from the standpoint of any

of the parties to the activity and this may include the participants, whether professional or lay, other people outside the
direct experience of the activity, such as relatives, or some
other organisation or group. In such studies, there is no guarantee of a consensus between these vantage points. The community at large may want the service user to behave quietly,
the professional may aspire for the service user to achieve
some kind of ultimate release from a problem or condition,
while the service user may want satisfaction in the here and
now.

Traditionally, psychologists undertaking outcome appraisal
may have looked in the direction of *attitude change* in the individual. The impact of an activity upon an individual may
depend on what sort of significant change is brought about.
Indeed, some would question the extent to which people's
attitudes, let alone their personalities, are amenable to such
changes. Another way of formulating the task involves focusing on the problem rather than on the person. However, this
requires that the problem itself can be defined in terms which
permit appraisal.

Answers to the following questions need to be found. How is
the problem specified? How will changes in its character and
intensity be measured? How can we be sure that such
changes are the direct consequences of the activity and do
not proceed from other as yet unconsidered factors?
(Lieberman and Bond, 1978, p. 225). The difficulty of research in this area is that before-and-after measurement is difficult or impossible since a person is likely to become involved
in an activity after the problem becomes difficult to handle. So
the appraisal cannot reach back to examine the individual in
her or his circumstances before involvement commenced
(Leiberman and Borman, 1976, p. 460). Whether the research is concerned with the group member or the problem,
the criteria for judging effectiveness are equally important.
These depend both on the way effectiveness is conceptualised
and also on the theoretical perspective of the person evaluating.

At what time will it be done?

Does the appraisal have to be complete yesterday (a common requirement in bureaucracies!), in the immediate future, or at some indeterminate date?

Such questions begin to shape the timing of data collection. Commonly, some form of appraisal will be called for in any activity where there is an element of statutory funding or a contract to provide a specified service. There may even be a regular process of review. In these circumstances, it is useful to develop guidelines for review and to ensure that the appraisal is compatible with them.

Over what period will it be done?

Will the appraisal be carried out over a short term, say two weeks, or over a long period, such as five years? Whereas much appraisal is, as they say, quick and dirty, sometimes service users and/or social workers may be able to justify to themselves, and possibly even to a funding person or other source, the idea of carrying out fairly lengthy study of the issues raised during the life of an activity. The disadvantage of this may be that the data and results will possess all those features of qualitative, open-ended research which irritate hard-nosed seekers after evaluative proof. The advantages include the possible ongoing interaction between insights gained about the processes of the activity and constant refining and re-conceptualisation which is stimulated by the research process itself. As was noted at the outset of this chapter, much appraisal involves continually going back and reformulating both the questions needing addressing and methods of addressing them.

Carrying out the appraisal

There are three main overlapping and often cyclically repeating stages involved in the appraisal process: reflecting, programming and doing the job, each of which involves particular tasks. We deal with the subsequent stage of producing and using the appraisal separately below.

Reflection

This begins before the appraisal has started and continues throughout. In settings where the activities change direction and character, or where qualitative methodology is used, the person doing the appraisal needs to be accustomed constantly to putting the entire research process under scrutiny and being prepared to shift objectives, change the emphasis and area of data collection, and rethink the analysis and projected outcomes. At the more bread-and-butter level, the process of reflection needs to focus on the data gathered.

Programming

There generally is a point where those involved in the appraisal feel able to make some practical plans and draw up some kind of programme. In the light of the previous paragraph, it is clear that while this needs to be firm enough to enable effective progress to be made, it should be sufficiently flexible to cope with necessary changes.

Doing the job

This stage involves translating the programme into action and making sure some kind of limits are set to the study. This latter point is important because there is a great temptation to devise research which is too grand ever to be achieved. The task needs to be kept manageable. To this end, it is very important to set some realistic *deadlines* for each stage of the process, and to stick to them.

   The procedure of carrying out a quantitative study may make it possible to separate out these stages fairly clearly. But in qualitative research, there is usually no clear point at which the collection of evidence ceases and the analysis begins. Often what happens is that the process of analysis begins as soon as the evaluator starts to pick over the evidence and draw some preliminary conclusions, to be fed back into further attempts to gather evidence. This process involves a continual spiral, so further reflection, reprogramming and data collection may continue right to the end of the study.

In the final phase, there is always the need to consider what will happen if the outcome of the research is not a happy ending. For instance, appraisal of women's consciousness-raising groups has highlighted the divergence between them and other helping groups, in respect of their impact on women's problems. A striking contrast exists between the symptom reduction achieved in psychotherapy and the lack of impact of consciousness-raising groups on people's symptoms. Rather than the emphasis in consciousness-raising groups being upon a specific outcome, their impact may be evident in members' general increased self- esteem and self-worth (Lielemn *et al.*, 1981, p. 595).

Producing and using the appraisal

In this last stage, the stakeholders will all need to play their proper part – service users, workers, managers and others. If all has gone reasonably well, though not necessarily according to plan as we have seen above, there will be something to report back to others. This is an important stage. Far too often, the results of research stay in someone's filing cabinet as 'that brilliant study I will write up some day when there is time'. Provided the above cautions have been heeded, the scope of the study is kept modest and the deadlines have been adhered to, the main skill required now is the assertiveness and confidence actually to commit oneself to sharing the results with others, either in written form or by face to face meetings with them. How it is done does not matter as much as ensuring that it happens!

The usefulness of appraisal: a caution

The key question here from the vantage point of the evaluator is how relevant, reliable, comprehensive or systematic the evidence is. This depends on how successfully the above questions have been addressed.

From the vantage point of the person involved in empowerment, the key question may be whether or not the appraisal is going to contribute to the future life of the activity, or sabotage it. From the viewpoint of rigorous research, effective appraisal depends on the evaluator satisfying a number of important criteria, including reliability, validity, comparability with other appraisals and relevance to the population being evaluated. Empowering activities are just as prone as any other aspects of social work, to all the problems raised by trying to meet these criteria.

On the whole, there is little indication from evaluative research that self-help and user-led initiatives can be proved to benefit participants. But that reflects more on the lack of serious research than it indicates that participants do not gain from activities. Nor does it appear to prevent people taking part and appearing to gain a good deal from these activities. Within the field of self-help more attention has been paid to tackling the appraisal of groupwork that anything else. In this respect, the lack of proof of outcome effectiveness does not contrast particularly with other aspects of groupwork. For example, the popularity of sensitivity-oriented groups has not been lessened by the general lack of research indicating that they have any beneficial results (Back, 1972, p. 14).

From the standpoint of service users, it is necessary to bear in mind the likelihood that rigorous appraisal will suggest that not all the outcomes of self-help will be positive. After all, there is evidence to this effect. Consciousness-raising groups may have adverse effects on members. This is not because of any intrinsic problems of the individual, but reflects the all too common contradictory situation of women, who become more assertive and provoke negative responses from those who are surprised by their changed behaviour. As Annette Brodsky notes, in her research into consciousness-raising groups for women:

> In a parallel fashion to the sensitivity group member who expects others outside the group to respond as positively as the group, CR [consciousness-raising] group members often find that the group understands, but the outside world does not change to correspond with the groups' level of awareness. It is at this stage that women tend to become angry with their employers, lovers, and old friends for continuing to act in chauvinistic, stereotyped patterns. A new response from a woman may be either ignored, misunderstood, patronisingly laughed at, or invoke a threatened retaliatory confrontation . . . In frustration women may overreact and, as a result, provoke just the response they fear to get. For example, loud demands for better treatment on the job by a previously meek woman may well meet with a backlash response leading to termination of her entire job. (Brodsky, 1981, p. 576)

Some individuals may break down in psychoses or experience a range of less serious but significant traumas including the loss of their defences, with no substitute being provided (Back, 1972, p. 221). Women's consciousness-raising groups in the feminist movement have a distinctive history, relying on persuasion to maintain a political feminist ideology and avoid groups becoming therapeutic (Bond and Reibstein, 1979).

There is evidence that women joining consciousness-raising groups use psychotherapy more than the general population and that their motives for joining are not significantly associated with dissatisfaction with existing services (Lieberman, 1979, pp. 150–63). In the case of widows' groups, far from members coming together through dissatisfaction with inadequate professional services, groups possibly serve the function of remedying failed social networks and do not serve a population coterminous with the client groups of professionals (Bankoff, 1979, pp. 192–3). In an evaluative study of fifteen women's consciousness-raising groups, Lieberman *et al.* (1979, pp. 356–61) found that most seemed to have a limited though useful therapeutic value and did not reduce the problems of women or encourage personal growth as did encounter groups. On the other hand, women gained an enhanced perspective on their circumstances. The researchers concluded that consciousness-raising is no substitute for therapy for women with chronic or severe problems and may not change their lifestyles, but it enables mildly depressed people to revise and improve their self-image.

Evidence from other areas of empowerment corroborates this view that it may not be fruitful to judge the outcome of group activities in such simple terms as problem reduction. In an appraisal of the impact of a medical self-help group, Videka (1979, p. 386) found that its value lay in helping people to manage their problems and maintain their sense of self-worth rather than in changing them or encouraging introspection or interpersonal learning. In general, then, there is no proof that self-help activities will benefit participants. On the contrary, there are indications that some people experiencing some kinds of groups may be harmed.

Possible products of appraisal

Will the outcome of appraisal be simply used for personal reflection? Will it lead to the sharing of experiences simply between participants in the empowering activity? Will some form of report be written, summarising the findings of the appraisal? For which audience will it be written? Will the appraisal be used by professionals, service users, students or the general reader?

Will the product be a formal summary of survey findings or questionnaire results, or a case study in the form of pen-pictures? To what extent will the product be tailored to the requirements of some external demand, such as the need to justify continued funding? Will this mean that the product is more of a public relations exercise than an objective, critical study?

The reality is that the needs of most activities are likely to be met best by a series of different sorts of products at different times for different purposes and audiences. A plan based on that tactic would seem more suitable than the idea of a single mammoth work, produced years after everybody has long gone who was connected with the activity (or, more likely by that stage, perpetually in a state of revision and never finally published at all).

The most appropriate point to leave the appraisal is at the point where the social worker is considering, in the same careful way as at the outset, how to *feed back the findings*. This process needs to involve service users as centrally as it did when the preparations for the appraisal were being made. Absolutely essential to this process, of course, is the issue of who owns the appraisal document, what control the service users have over its content, and what their power is to nego-tiate changes in it, or even to veto statements with which they may disagree Finally, what provision is there for the service users to contribute their own comments to the appraisal? This is the moment of truth, in which the power relationships between participants in an empowering activity may be laid bare.

In conclusion, here is a checklist of the main stages, and within each, some key question and issues which needs to be considered:

Overview of the process of appraisal

The major stages are as follows: clarifying the task, preparing for the appraisal, carrying it out and producing and using its products. It should be remembered that far from each stage being completed before the next is begun, in practice con-stant 'looping back' will normally be necessary, to revise the task of appraisal and its implementation.

The Process of Empowering Evaluation

Clarifying the task

- What is the purpose of this evaluation?
- Whom will this evaluation empower?
- Do all stake holders control the evaluation?
- What sort of evaluation is sought?
- Is a critical appraisal/case-study approach preferred?

Preparing for the appraisal

- Collecting information
- Identifying sources of information
- Specifying what evidence will be collected
- Anticipating problems of information gathering
- Programming at what time it will be done
- Scheduling the supply of the resources to the evaluation

Carrying out the appraisal

- Reflection
- Programming
- Doing the job

Producing and using the appraisal

Ensuring products of the appraisal meet needs.

9

Professionals and Service Users: An Empowering Relationship?

Introduction

The advent of the paradigm of empowerment has increased the likelihood that the relationship between social workers and service users, already fraught with complex issues, will be inherently problematic. At the heart of this issue are the tensions between the relatively powerful practitioner and the relatively powerless service user, in the context of the overall goal of developing an empowering practice. This chapter examines first some of the cautions and subsequently some pointers towards effective relationships between them.

Cautions

In this first part of the chapter, we summarise the major areas of risk to the activities of both service users and professionals, focusing on user-led and self-help activities in particular: namely, the inherently problematic relationship between professionals and service users; ways in which each party may retreat from, or corrupt the challenge thereby posed; and finally the difficulties of handling the element of power in the relationship.

161

Service users and social workers: a problematic relationship

Once the consent of the user of social work or social services to the way she or he is dealt with can no longer be taken for granted, then the so-called 'proper' relationship between the social worker and the service user becomes problematic. Or rather, it was always problematic, only highlighting it in this way means that now it cannot be ignored. In any case, there has been evidence for some time that, clients apart, social workers have not even developed relationships with non-professional helpers to their full potential (Holme and Maizels, 1978). Further, it may be that the worker will tend to hold clients responsible in one way or another for this state of affairs; things are 'not what they used to be' in the agency. Social workers are not treated with respect 'like they were in the old days'. They are less likely to be thanked by their clients than attacked, verbally through criticism, or even, physically assaulted.

For reasons of maintaining accountability, not just to the State and to professional values but also to service users, it is all to the good that in contemporary social work service users are increasingly likely to question such autonomy and authority as the practitioner possesses (Haug and Sussman, 1969, p. 154). Also, the mistakes of social workers and the areas of their practice which may be less than ideal are more and more likely to be the subjects of critical scrutiny, not only by clients but by other professionals, the media and the general public.

Resistance by service users to the exercise of power by social workers may be passive. They may opt out or refuse to co-operate. Or it may be active, in which case they may exercise their rights in terms of the Children Act 1989 or the NHS and Community Care Act 1990, for instance, and complain. Or they may petition, sit-in, strike, riot or contact a lawyer. Service users may also doubt that social workers have the requisite knowledge to deal with them effectively and may claim the right to define the problem and subsequently to determine not to call upon the social worker but simply to try and manage their own problems.

If we locate the post-war popularity of self-help or user-led groups in the context of such disillusionment with social services on the part of the service user, then the character of user-led movements takes on a critical dimension. Far from our being able to dismiss user-led initiative, as largely the middle-class playing at alternative therapies or as a reactionary shift away from State support and towards self-support, they emerge, in part at least, as a sign of the consumer revolt against some forms of social work.

So we need to treat with caution any indications that social workers are negotiating with the user-led field. The issue is not whether they are being useful, but whether they are colonising, invading, or inappropriately interfering. Baistow notes that Bell specifies that user empowerment in psychotherapy would involve professionals in mental health services giving up some of their expert power (Bell, 1989, quoted in Baistow, 1994, p. 38); this shift sits uneasily alongside the appropriation of empowerment by many professionals as simply another task for them, through such contemporary fashions as new careerists, aides, lay helpers, volunteers, to say nothing of facilitating user-led groups (Ward and Mullender, 1992).

Consumer control: a false promise? We need now to locate the dynamic between the worker and the service user of social work in its organisational context. At first sight, Dumont's exposition of the 'new fact of professionalism' (Dumont, 1972) complements the growing popularity of self-help in social work and offers optimism about the capacity of governments and agencies for social change. Dumont identifies six principles in the new fact of professionalism: consumer control, indifference to credentials, a sense of common language and purpose transcending individual professional practice, a critical attitude, impatience with the pace of change, and an investment in political activity.

'*Meta-professionalism*' The last three of these principles are unexceptionable to many professionals, and the third – what amounts to meta-professionalism – has been around in social work in Britain, in Intermediate Treatment for instance (Adams, 1976), for many years. But it can be argued first that the extent of the new professionalsm is exaggerated by Dumont and that it is restricted to students and influential people as well as members of some reforming movements; second, that its influence is likely to be limited; third, that if the new professionalism implies that professionals should not claim exclusive rights over any distinctive knowledge and skills, then this is a spurious argument for non-professionalism.

Retreat by professionals from the challenge

The implementation of the National Health Service and Community Care Act 1990, however, has given legislative force in Britain to the part played by the voluntary and informal sectors alongside the statutory and private sectors, in providing health and social care services. In the face of this growing participation by users in the voluntary and informal sectors, three forms of retreat by professionals are likely: professional complacency may be reinforced, professionals as service providers may opt out, or self-help or user-led activities may retreat into alternativism.

Reinforcing professional complacency While self-help or user-led groups could be dismissed as having no discernible impact on the user group served by existing statutory services, this is too simple and inaccurate a denunciation. It is true that some groups may actually support the political status quo and that if there is any serious threat to invade the territorial power-base of professional activities in local authorities at any rate, there might be some significant legal battles (Robinson and Henry, 1977, p. 136). But there are some striking examples of self-help or user-led activities impinging on those statutory services without themselves coming under threat. At one end of the continuum, there are activities involving empowered carers and self-carers as part of a pattern of community care provision; at the other end, there are empowered users acting independently of professionals.

The reality, however, is that the threat to the quality of helping services and activities is more insidious. In the health field, it has been observed that most self-help or user-led groups hold the same view of health and illness as do more conventional helpers (Robinson and Henry, 1977, p. 126). In the activities they studied, Robinson and Henry found that the focus is upon helping individual people with problems rather than upon the broader structural features of the situation in which they live, such as the problems of homelessness, overcrowding, loneliness, stress, and so on. In such circumstances, self-help or user-led activities actually may make more pronounced the very health problems they seek to alleviate (Robinson and Henry, 1977, p. 126), by meeting immediate needs, deluding people into thinking that local action will solve their problems, diverting people from seeking their proper share of potential services and giving officials and agencies an excuse to neglect the provision that is due to people.

A further consequence may be to exacerbate a split between caring and technical aspects of medical practice. Using the example of the Cancer Aftercare and Rehabilitation Society (CARE), Robinson and Henry suggest that because the cancer patient is given regular checks, the work of CARE begins by picking up the emotional needs of the patient. Self-help or user-led groups may thus simply follow on and reinforce the existing direction of professional practice, in the less technical and challenging or critical areas (Robinson and Henry, 1977, p. 128). But as the authors acknowledge, reducing the scope of professional activities to the technical area could be seen as positive, because thereby their power is circumscribed and to a degree limited.

Opting out by agencies   Co-operation in the form of working partnerships between paid social workers and volunteers, or interweaving of statutory and voluntary services, may be welcomed in principle. But care needs to be taken that the participation of users, for example, through self-help is not seen as a way of cutting costs by the erosion of statutory services (Darvill and Munday, 1984, p. 5). The paid worker and the volunteer both have distinctive contributions to make to services and each may enrich what the other provides. The introduction of the mixed economy of provision in community care has not made more secure the state provision of resources underpinning the work of volunteers, carers and self-carers. The greater the tendency for government to argue for retrenchment in the responsibility of the state for people's welfare, the more there is a risk that budget cuts will be made progressively and more swiftly in areas of work where people seem to be developing the ability to help themselves and each other. This presents professionals with the need to work out strategies for defending the self-help or user-led field against negative consequences of its very successes, and ensuring the appropriate measures are taken by agency providers to build in resourcing for the voluntary and informal sectors.

Alternativism: danger or opportunity?   The rationales for self-help or user-led activity seem to imply that it flourishes when disenchantment with existing services and associated supporting organisations and networks is running high. But more than that, self-help or user-led activity may be infused with the distinct but often connected strains of alternativism or even anti-professionalism. This is not to deny that many professionals themselves may allow, facilitate, encourage, participate in or even stimulate, self-help or user-led activities. But sometimes action by service users – as in the campaigns of 1994–5 to establish legislation promoting disabled people's rights – goes hand in hand with antagonism towards an individualistic, privatised, competitive social environment, which disempowers people rather than giving them power to allocate adequate resources to the services they choose and need. In general, the more rooted in genuine empowerment the activity, the more tenuous and potentially conflict-ridden its links with professional workers are likely to be.

There is nothing intrinsically wrong with adopting an anti-professional stance. But the consequences of standing off from contact with professionals may be a retreat into alternative activity rather than maintaining a constant debate with the professional world and continually challenging existing practice. One problem with the self-help and user-led field may be that to the extent that professionals are able to dismiss it as merely another alternative, it may lose its power to act as a critic of what social workers, health visitor, doctors and nurses do. Those who retreat to an alternative position should not be criticised for it. It could be that professionals have treated them perfunctorily once too often, which is a pity when it happens. Social workers ignore criticism from service users at their peril.

Corruption by professionals of the challenge

The relationship between social workers and service users is vulnerable to corruption from three directions: exploitation, professionalism or co-option of service users as non-professionals.

Exploitation of non-professionals There is a risk that service users may be seen just as another kind of volunteer. At the start of this chapter, we noted how the potential benefits of volunteers have not been realised by social workers. On the whole, in Britain in the past the main role of volunteers working with professional social workers has been in befriending and practical services, while in the probation service they have been involved in befriending and counselling (Holme and Maizels, 1978, p. 88). Experience in New York of using indigenous non-professionals as aides in mental health has served the function of providing psychological first-aid and acting as a means of inervention in community health issues. Aides may thus improve service delivery and help to increase the understanding of mental health problems held by more traditional staff. In addition to providing direct services, community action and community education, it is suggested that aides may also take on the role of social planners (Hallowitz and Riessman, 1967). In Britain, in 1995 the government's plans for divorce law reform included an enhanced role for voluntary agencies such as Relate, in mediation services, working alongside solicitors and the court welfare service. But on the whole, non-professional helping continues to play a very restricted part in many professionals' working week.

The use of non-professionals should not be undertaken lightly. Here the word 'use' acquires significance in itself. In the New York example quoted above, some aides feared exploitation and felt relatively ignorant of basic skills such as routine recording. In this sense, Hallowitz's aides remain inescapably subservient, secondary in importance to, and dependent on, professionals.

Knight and Hayes advocate the use of non-professionals or indigenous workers, in the light of limited but encouraging research, indicating that

> non-professional or indigenous workers have a number of advantages over professionals. Living in the same neighbourhood, they do not commute, and have a knowledge of their locality that can only come from living there. They are of the same social class as those they are trying to help, do not have narrowly defined professional roles, and can offer friendship rather than just a service, they are less threatening to local people because they do not have elements of control or power, or the association with the state, that workers in official social work agencies have. (Knight and Hayes, 1981, p. 96)

They admit that indigenous workers do tend to take on too much work and risk burning out, but that proper professional support can alleviate this.

Professionalisation of service users Self-help or user-led activities may be prone to the insidious process of professionalising the participants. To understand this, we need to distinguish between the kind of wisdom acquired by professionals and the experiential wisdom gained by self-helpers or service-users. At the point where members achieve control over their own problems they are in a position to manage aspects of their own lives independently from the practice of professionals. But it has been observed that many health care groups fail to capitalise on this opportunity. They do not work out the implications of the power they possess. The consequence is that group members give themselves help which does not differ significantly from that offered them by professionals. The only difference is that they are administering it themselves (Robinson and Henry, 1977, p. 129).

Co-option by professionals The biggest threat to self-help or user-led activities is of a takeover by professional practice. Takeovers may occur in any setting where the power of one group over a market is affected by the existence of successful competitors. The more effective self-help or user-led activities become, the more they are at risk of co-option by professionals. Self-appointed experts, media personalities, researchers, writers and practitioners in many fields appear from time to time, riding on the backs of service users. Professionals can make only a limited contribution to self-help or user-led endeavours before they begin to take over and reduce other people's belief in their ability to break out of constraints and empower themselves.

But in spite of these risks, there is room for optimism, especially in the case of the more resilient self-help or user-led activity. Marieskind's observation on women's groups probably has wider relevance:

> Despite the vulnerability to co-option, the self-help group is an invaluable concept. It is not just a personal solution for individual women's needs – although that alone is a valid reason for its ex-

istence. The self-help group is a tool for inducing collective thought and action, and radical social change. (Marieskind, 1984, pp. 31–2)

The gains from collaboration between professionals and service users may be counterbalanced by the potential dangers. Service users may gain credibility, support and resources from professional help, but may sacrifice independence. Kleiman *et al.* (1976) records some of the hazards of partnerships between users and professionals. In the American Cancer Society project examined by Kleiman, professionals tended to criticise helpers for their lack of such counselling skills and volunteers did not have the motivation and assertiveness to take charge of the running of the project themselves. Kleiman concludes depressingly:

> Can a self-help group find happiness within an agency? We must answer that it cannot. The growing popularity of this approach leads to hasty attempts to transplant a few features of self-help groups to the alien environment of an agency setting. Inevitably, the arbitrary extraction of self-help principles from the nurturant and supportive milieu of the group invites failure: the auto-immune systems of the host agency work to reject the graft. The bureaucratic directives and structural constraints imposed by agencies contravene the entire purpose and meaning of self-help – *leadership from below.* (Kleiman *et al.*, 1976, p. 409, emphasis in original)

It is difficult to predict the outcome of challenges by service users to professional knowledge and power. It is very unlikely that they will lead to the total dismantling of such professional autonomy as social workers possess and more likely that the consequence will be a restriction of professional authority to the most limited and esoteric elements of the knowledge base (Haug and Sussman, 1969, p. 159). Initiatives by service users are capable of growing through the redefinition of this uncertain territory between professionals and clients.

The problems of power

We have noted that the power component of the relationship between social workers and non-professional service users is very significant, hence now we identify four specific dangers: playing power games, toning down the intensity of the self-help or user-led experience, fragmentation of non-professional interests, and threats to social workers by expert service users.

Playing power games to avoid empowering service users Is the power imbalance between professionals and service users immune to pressure from the user to democratise service planning and provision in the managed markets of health and social care? There is a risk that tokenistic activity by professionals may result merely in formal nodding to principles such as user participation. It is significant that behind many debates about the relationships between providers and service users of social services lies the issue of *power*. The self-help field tends to espouse the principle of power sharing between professional and lay helpers and many social workers accept as normal the principles of openness of communication with, and accessibility to, clients and even a devolution of skills to clients and service users in areas formerly regarded as a professional monopoly. It is in this light that Hurvitz comments that 'unconditional regard for another is not a skill or property of a professionally trained person. Stupid lovers can demonstrate it . . . and it can be demonstrated by group members for each other' (Hurvitz, 1974, p. 106). The ultimate demystification involves encouraging service users to realize that helping skills can be acquired like other skills.

Toning down the intensity of the self-help or user-led experience Advocacy can be fudged and self-advocacy may remain a gleam in the eye. User empowerment may be implemented in a tokenistic fashion, the anger of service users or their dissatisfaction with existing services defused through protracted negotiation or some other bureaucratic process. The critical perspective of service users on the services with which they have been in contact may have been blunted in the process.

The anger of service users may be translated into respectable language, their style proceduralised and their language sanitised. Professionals may play a part, deliberately or unwittingly, in socialising them in the proper procedures for gaining access to resources and skills which will empower them.

In all this, there is the constant danger that self-help will run out of steam and function like the professional service. In consequence, service users lose the chance to share in management. Admittedly, this may not be the fault solely of the professionals. Within the service users' camp there may be factions. Some may want to imitate professional practice without appreciating that others prefer to plough the more difficult but, for them, fertile furrow of consumerism. Among service users, too, the assertive may advocate for others, removing their scope for self-advocacy. There is no reason why among service users there should be any more homogeneity of beliefs than exists among professionals.

Fragmentation of non-professional interests   When we compare the circumstances of workers in agencies with those of service users, it is easy to see that in areas such as health and social care, the professional workers are a concentrated interest with plenty of continuity built into their relatively powerful position. In contrast, most service users are in a dispersed situation. That is, they have relatively slight chances of meeting to develop a common approach to negotiating with professionals. How often do groups of people meet to compare notes on their visits to the same out-patients' clinic, general practitioners' surgery or social services office? It is hard to consider how we would set about the logistic task or organising this, let alone how we would persuade professionals and service users alike of its desirability.

A consequence of the way helping services are organised and delivered is that each self-help or user-led activity tends to function in isolation from others, unless it is afflicated to a common organisational base. In the health field, this tendency for people to get on with the running of their own activities has been noted, along with the consequence that far from the fact of different self-help or user-led groups joining forces to deal with common problems, they often are fragmented by divergences of local beliefs and practice, competitiveness and petty squabbles (Robinson and Henry, 1977, p. 130).

Threats to social workers by expert service users From the viewpoint of hard-pressed social workers, insecure about their professional credibilty, there may be conflict between enjoying the superior status and omniscience invested in them by having non-professional service users working alongside them, and the anxiety that this cannot be lived up to. There is also the potential conflict between keenness to see non-professionals develop skills, reluctance to hand over to them responsibility and autonomy, and anxiety that non-professionals, however unwittingly, will do damage.

It is possible also that relationships between professionals and service users highlight the threat posed by the more active and immediate response of the expert lay practitioner to client need, in contrast with the more deliberately assessed and planned course of the professional's intervention. It is also probable, of course, that the non-professional has more time to do a thorough job of supporting a fellow member of a self-help or user-led group than a hard-pressed social worker. There is no doubt that the informal practices of many a self-help or user-led group reinforce spontaneity and informality and pose a threat to the professional who relies on traditional communications and lines of authority. There is a sense in which this caricatures, but illustrates, the potential difficulties of bridging the gap between the professional's traditional methods and style and those of the service user. Naturally, when the association between service user and social worker prospers it brings advantages, such as the enthusiasm and conviction service users bring to their activities and the encouragement they may give to professionals to experiment with new methods.

Empowering relationships between service users and social workers

In the second part of this chapter, a number of general principles are advanced, as the foundation for an empowering relationship between social work and self-help or user-led activities in a locality.

Empowerment should be mutual Essentially, the ideal relationship between social workers and service users would be one in which each witnessed, and possibly contributed actively towards, the empowerment of the other. This is far easier to set down on paper than it is to achieve in practice.

Optimism should be cultivated

In a survey of the views of mental health professionals about self-help groups, Levy (1976, p. 311) found that whilst over 46 per cent thought self-help groups had an important part to play in a comprehensive mental health service, less than a third saw it as likely that their agency would be interested in integrating self-help activities with the services they provided. However, the findings of Levy's survey confirms the view of Lieberman and Borman that on the whole self-help activities are viewed by service users as complementary with, rather than antagonistic towards, professionals (Levy, 1982, p. 1273).

   The desired relationship between professionals and service users is defined fundamentally by whether the service users view their activity as integral, facilitated or autonomous in relation to professionals. If the latter, then there is little more to be said, since they will not want professionals involved in their activities, and this stance must be respected by professional workers themselves. However, in the case of integral or facilitated activities, service users and professionals may each gain from contact, and Judy Wilson (1986, pp. 84–95) points out many of these benefits. For service users they include resources such as meeting places, administrative help and transport, publicity, extra help through volunteers and students and credibility through the use of an agency address. For professionals the gains may be increased knowledge about the needs of service users and the chance to improve services thereby.

Non-compromising professional support

Undoubtedly there is a need for self-help or user-led activities to retain a degree of autonomy appropriate to their circumstances. While users may benefit from learning how to build effective links with existing professional services, it is not in their interest to be taken over and incorporated into such services. As a consequence they could lose their independent identity and much of their creative enthusiasm (Tyler, 1976, p. 447). Relations between service users and professionals should be seen as tender and nurtured accordingly. In Liz Evans's study of self-help groups of parents of children with disabilities, she found that professionals could react defensively when parents started becoming enthusiastic and assertive about care. In fact, suspicion tended to be mutual. Whilst newsletters from carers to professionals helped to inform them about what was happening, in the two groups where problems did not arise three factors may have contributed: first, the fact that groups already existed in their areas and had prepared professionals to be more accepting, second, the existence of co-ordinated leadership by groups with experience, and third, the greater care taken in preparation for joint meetings between parents and psychotherapists (Evans *et al.*, 1986, p. 43).

Clarifying the basis of work between social workers and service users

We can build on Phyllida Parsloe's extremely useful paper (Parsloe, 1986, p. 13) in which she identifies three social work skills: ensuring clients understand the political as well as the personal nature of their problems, that this is communicated adequately to managers, councillors and the public at large, and that the level of social services are defended. This leads to what Parsloe calls a 'professional anti-professional' approach (Parsloe, 1986, p. 14), which includes seeing clients as departmental resources in the context of creating open and sharing relationships with them and advocating both for them and on behalf of the personal social services. In pursuit of this, there is a reciprocal need for social policy to support self-help efforts, through legislation. Consultative personnel and skills should also be made available, as well as the willingness to liaise with and facilitate activity, without threatening to take it over.

Sol Tax (Tax, 1976, p. 450) argues that if traditional primary groups like the family, church and neighbourhood were given more support there would not be such a vacuum left by the withering of these, for the new self-help groups to fill. Tax is less sure about the value or organising self-help in say, a Bureau of Self-help Groups Affairs, since self-help should begin with a level of awareness in the community itself which simply encourages groups to develop as they wish. Whatever we feel about Tax's value judgement concerning the vulnerability of primary groups in the modern world, it is undeniable that people involved in self-help which relates in one way or another to professional activities should have access to appropriate sources of support, resources, consultation and so on, without in the process having to compromise essential elements of their position in the self-help field.

In effect, the clarification of this relationship between professional workers and service users should enable the social worker to sort out more rigorously and effectively the distinctive roles which need to be adopted in a range of settings. In some of these, professionals are kept more at arm's length than in others, ensuring in the process the preservation of the empowered status of service users.

Real empowerment

Quite simply, social workers should be aware of the tendency to delegate rather than to hand over real power. The acid test is the willingness to give service users the actual resources to do the job themselves. In this area, tokenism is to be deplored.

Opportunities of localism

To be effective, self-help activity needs to be a collaboration with professionals which recognises the distinctive contribution which service users can make.

Tony Gibson's thesis is that small-scale, local grassroots action groups are an antidote to the bureaucratic strangulation which afflicts our centralised society (Gibson, 1979, p. 15). He argues that, contrary to popular belief, ordinary people without skills, special training or even the confidence to do it, can take a lead and run such groups (Gibson, 1979, p. 17). He points out that in the process the relationship between professionals and lay people may need to be redefined in favour of the latter (Gibson, 1979, p. 128). Perhaps a degree of training, support and resources to underpin such activity should be negotiated where possible, though, from social work agencies.

Community-based methods of organisation

It is accepted that there is a need not to fixate on the notion of community-based and patch-based social work as panaceas for practice. However, some extremely useful principles can be itemised as a basis for more detailed development in the light of local circumstances. Drawing on a BASW paper

(BASW, 1984, p. 14) Roger Hadley's book (Hadley *et al.*, 1987) and work by Gawlinski (Gawlinski, and Graessle 1988), we can assert the need for social workers to respect the user's perspective in all their work and build up their understanding of local networks and relationships. Additionally, it is important to try to achieve a broad concept of teamwork, including in the team a greater mix of people, such as aides, volunteers and service users. Social workers engaging with user-led initiatives should avoid the temptation to incorporate service users wholesale into the professional framework of activity.

Whether or not the patch approach is taken as appropriate, the implementation of the NHS and Community Care Act 1990 heightens the general need for social workers to support and maintain the strength of other professional services, voluntary agencies and the informal sector in their locality, rather than either undermining them or handing over to them certain tasks whilst withdrawing from the responsibilities of adequately resourcing them. Bamford indentifies seven useful principles inherent in Hadley and McGrath's (1980) approach to community-based social work:

- locally based teams focusing on small areas or patches
- the capacity to obtain detailed information about the patch
- accessibility and acceptability to the patch population
- close liaison with other local agencies and groups
- integration of all field and domiciliary services within patch teams
- participative management
- substantial autonomy exercised by patch teams. (Bamford, 1982, p. 96).

Building on to the statutory, informal and voluntary sectors

The NHS and Community Care Act 1990 strengthens the argument that the relationship between user-led activities, as part of the informal sector of social care, and the voluntary sector should be symbiotic (Wolfenden, 1978, p. 28). The voluntary sector generally offers a less bureaucratic and a more flexible means of support and encouragement than do many agencies in the statutory sector. Some user-led activities which lack any other formal organisational connections or reference points of their own, will welcome the support offered by a voluntary body and may even prefer it to a link with a statutory agency.

This involves the informal as well as the voluntary sectors. Self-help and mutual aid in work with older people, for example, involves relatives and carers as well as elderly people themselves. More often than not, it is the carers who initiate schemes to meet the needs of relatives and/or close friends. At this juncture, the process of helping elderly people is furthered by networks of individuals, groups and organisations which exemplify the inter-connectedness of formal and informal patterns of caring in the community. An obvious area for self-help initiatives to develop is in the support of those who care for confused elderly relatives. On the one hand, this may be viewed positively as enriching sources of support in the informal sector. Alternatively, it may be seen as one consequence of public policy leaving many carers for the elderly, and women in particular, unsupported at home, looking after them.

Although health and social care agencies have responsibility for providing community care, often the burden of quality control, that is, ensuring that the service to the user *feels* adequate, rests on carers and service users themselves. That is, provided informal carers seem to be coping, community care professionals may let well alone and simply adopt a rationing approach, by allocating scarce resources elsewhere. In this sense, while the responsibility for services may rest with management in the organisation, the task of verifying good social work experiences is left with the service user and carer. But social workers should not accept this state of affairs complacently. Bamford has identified their responsibilities, arguing that the role of social services is 'that of supporting voluntary care, of providing direct care for those who need it, and of recognising the importance of breaking down barriers between the community and the professionals. Translating these concepts into practice requires a radical shift in professional attitudes' (Bamford, 1982, p. 96).

Profane practice

If professional services exemplify the sacred principles of practice, then initiatives by service users and carers perhaps need to express something profane. It is unfortunate that we have to make the point in this fashion, rather than in reverse, since self-help should be capable of acting as the reciprocal to whatever services exist, rather than simply as a radical alternative.

Progress in this area depends on the ability of social workers to avoid the risk their client will slide further into poverty and need. We can agree with Balloch that people need jobs and relief from poverty and isolation rather than exhortations to help themselves (Balloch *et al.*, 1985, pp. 105–5). However, it is necessary to reach beyond the vague exhortation to practitioners to engage in action to improve the social environment in which service users live. Phyllida Parsloe (1986) argues that social work should avoid escaping into individualisation, privatisation or bureaucratisation, from the social and political issues which surround practice in the community. Perhaps the same point can be made of the area of user empowerment, which needs to avoid the twin dangers of becoming either the preserve of a few relatively well-off middle-class, articulate people, or a substitute for professional services, as people care for themselves and each other.

Facilitation by social workers needs to be purposeful

There is no doubt that many self-help activities exist which perform a useful function for their members. However, the following illustration serves as a caution against involvement in a situation in the absence of adequate information about what it actually can offer service users and social workers.

A survey of active members of Recovery, a large self-help organisation in the US, with many affiliated groups, found that the typical member was a middle-class, middle-aged, moderately educated married woman with a husband in non-manual work (Wechsler, 1960, p. 302). Most had not had extensive histories of hospitalisation, over half had none, and a fifth had no professional treatment at all before joining Recovery. This coincides with the aim of the organisation's facilitator, to recruit those with relatively mild mental health problems. As many as a third had been members for one to two years and a further third for three years or more, a third of all members saying they no longer needed to attend. This indicates the social function performed for members by many self-help groups. However, it should be borne in mind that the support offered by the organisation may not be available from any other source. In fact, Recovery exemplifies the situation of the well-established self- help group or organisation, which may be looked to by potential members and professionals as capable of dealing with problems at an intensity comparable with established agencies. But in fact organisations like this cannot do so, since members tend not to be screened on entry, nor are leaders sufficiently selected, trained or professionally supported to guarantee this.

Minimising the risk of professional colonisation

At the other extreme from leaving people alone with their burden of self-care and care for others, there is a risk that professionals will take over activities and co-opt service users. In the process, professionals may exploit self-help or user-led initiatives while seeming to promote them, keeping themselves at the centre of the stage in the process. It is difficult for social workers to provide just sufficient leadership to enable the self-help or user-led activity to develop, yet not so much that service users are swamped.

Ensuring blurring of professional and self-help or user roles

Undoubtedly there is an ambiguity about the balance of power between professionals and service users in many facilitated situations. But this is no more problematic than the ambiguous situations of many participants themselves. For example, there is no denying that it was hard for Doctor Mowrer, starting his first self-help therapy Integrity Group in a mental hospital, to open with the comment that he too had been a patient in a mental hospital. But this cannot deny the reality of his professional position at the point the group started (Mowrer, 1984, p. 108). Mowrer also expresses more general ambivalence, symptomatic of activity in this field. On one hand he suggests that in the mental health field the stimulus for self-help comes as strongly as it ever did from the grassroots rather than from professionals (Mowrer, 1984, p. 145). Yet he acknowledges Lieberman and Borman's comment that many groups have had significant professional involvement in their inception and development (Mowrer, 1984, p. 143).

Although social workers may play a part as intiators, once it gets going, the activity remains largely managed and carried out by service users themselves. Social work support is thus likely to be more intermittent and the level of resourcing much less than in situations where user activity is an integral part of service provision, rather than standing outside it. But the central feature of empowerment is the type of facilitating leadership provided by the social worker. It should be emphasised that empowering activities which are facilitated in their early stages, later may become autonomous as participants acquire the necessary resources, skills and confidence. Professionals need to develop the skills to manage the tensions involved in providing services for people where appropriate, without slackening commitment to the overarching goal of empowering them.

10

Towards an Empowering Social Work

Introduction

This book has provided a framework for understanding the idea of empowerment, and knowledge about the skills required for developing the paradigm of empowerment-in-practice. Empowerment is a concept which may apply first and foremost to oneself, then to other individuals, groups and organisations in society. Or, it can be applied so as to enable workers, service users, carers and other people to further their own development and that of others. But this book has emphasised that in today's world, the personal and social aspirations of social workers and service users towards empowerment are unlikely to be realised in full, if at all. It is better to work in this spirit of cautious realism, than to set out with grandiose hopes which are quickly dashed.

This concluding chapter deals with the implications of the foregoing chapters and summarises the main issues which arise from the consideration of the framework set out in Chapter 2. It also considers the furthering of policies which espouse empowerment, in the political climate of the 1990s, with its emphasis on the creation of quasi or managed markets in health and welfare. We shall begin with a brief reference to this wider political context, since social work cannot segregate itself from the consequences of political realities for people's lives.

Changing context of politics and welfare policies

The broader social policy context in which empowering social work is practised is one in which the managed markets for the purchase and provision of health and social care have become firmly established. Whatever the detail of future changes in the balance between public, private, voluntary and informal sectors in what is often called the mixed economy of community care, there is little doubt that the mixture will persist in some form for the foreseeable future.

To the extent that empowerment is reflected in the social policies espoused by the Conservative Government since 1979, it is based on consumerist rather than participative assumptions about the situation of service users. In another sense, empowerment may be viewed as a rhetorical gesture in the direction of meeting the wishes of the service user in particular areas of need. The rhetoric of community care, for example, is about empowerment. But is the development of market-based health and social care provision actually likely to empower service users? From the viewpoint of the conservative government, in power from 1979 through the implementation of the market approach in the 1990s, empowering the service user means giving the consumer more choice. There is a significant gap between this view of empowerment and the approach which advocates enhancing the participation of the empowered service user in a democratised health and social care sector.

A political agenda beyond empowering individuals

Whatever social policies are adopted by the government, empowering individual service users is no substitute for developing and providing the professional services people need, as a whole. That is, focusing on making a person feel better by increasing awareness of social and personal circumstances is no substitute for mobilising empowering work in other domains. Additionally, no amount of work can relieve some people of the pain of their situations. This is not to underestimate the ways in which people may use their responses – both intellect and emotions – to contribute to their empowerment. But, there needs to be some connection between feeling empowered and actions to improve material circumstances. The following caution by Stokes has some truth, across the entire field: 'Neither self-help nor preventative health measures can relieve people of the burden of illness and death. Self-care is merely a way to gain some control over this process and to manage, not overcome the disease' (Stokes, 1981, p. 108). We cannot be dismissive, though, about the value of enabling people to feel better, as the successes of well-established complementary therapies demonstrate. Individual empowerment may help people who have suffered the consequences of social or personal traumas to rebuild their confidence and hope. Knight and Hayes's comment on the inner city applies more generally:

> At present many have retreated from social action into the private world of home, family, and television, they feel powerless, and display the same signs of passivity that are sometimes found in people who have no hope, there is a need to turn this mood of oppression, anxiety, dependency into positive action . . . There are limits to what state agencies can do for inner city neighbourhoods. And since much of what they do, they do badly, there is a need to curtail some of their operations and hand them over to people who might do it better, more cheaply. (Knight and Hayes, 1981, p. 95)

Previously, we have charted some of the difficulties and provided some practice illustrations and advice regarding work in different domains to develop an empowering practice. In this final chapter, this advice is drawn together in a guide to action. This is undertaken in the realisation that the field is complex and activities are various. Further, many social work settings leave something to be desired in terms of empowering initiatives. Also, it is not pretentious to suggest that social workers should be pursuing excellence and that this involves promoting innovation, challenging unthinking perpetuation of bad working practices, taking risks, and so on. Finally, there is a necessity not to miss the point that many user-led initiatives we have described arise partly, if not wholly, from a dissatisfaction with professional services and from a feeling that service users had better do something themselves.

Thompson's dichotomy between empowerment and oppression oversimplifies but makes a useful point: 'the actions of social workers (and their agencies) are crucial in determining whether oppression is increased and strengthened or, alternatively, challenged and undermined through the process of empowerment' (Thompson, 1993, p. 156).

The foregoing chapters on empowerment-in-practice suggest some lessons for professionals in the field, which are grouped in the remainder of this chapter, in four categories: general issues, values, policies and resources.

General issues

Tokenism or real participation

Rhetoric about empowerment of people should be tested to ascertain whether it is tokenistic or backed up by action. Let us assume that the initiative is concerned with the introduction of a new service. The following checklist could form the basis of a monitoring exercise regarding the extent of empowerment in the initiative:

- Have service users been involved from the outset: for example, in drafting the questions to be posed/issues to be addressed?

- Do service users play a key role in assessing the situation?

- Do service users have a say in how the services are planned, managed and delivered?
- Have service users control (or are they consulted after the key areas are determined and the major decisions made) over the allocation of the resources?
- Do service users contribute centrally to the evaluation of service delivery?

Clarity about conditions for effective work

The worker should appreciate at the outset the conditions which influence empowering work. An early task is to assess the situation. The key factors which determine an integral approach arise from the nature of relevant agencies delivering social work services and the situations of consumers to deal with them.

The identity of activity in legal terms should be selected and specified with care. Legal and policy obstacles need to be minimised. Effective developments are predicated on effective means by which issues arising can be tackled quickly and effectively. Partnerships between statutory and voluntary organisations are becoming more common and in such cases the existence of adequate collaborative mechanisms is even more important. An adequate organisational base should be identified, with attention to a degree of neutrality in terms of physical location and agency support which guarantees the integrity of self-help activities. A successful pilot venture funded from another source may suffice to persuade potential resourcers to support the venture.

The specification of focus of the activity should be done with care, in order to minimise the risk of likelihood of failure through dilution of effort or lack of clarity about what is being undertaken. Throughout, social workers should appreciate the paradox of empowerment, which if not handled properly may involve the patronising process of offering people back power they possessed before professionals became involved, rather than working with people in a genuinely empowering way.

Recognition of empowerment as a personal and a collective process

Empowerment-in-practice occupies different domains simultaneously. It concerns the personal growth and development of the individual as well as the ways groups of people engage collectively in self-help activities. It is mistaken, and may be totally stultifying, to see empowerment as a single one-dimensional process, or as something in which individuals engage, apart from others. Further, the reflexive nature of empowerment means that experience of the process will stimulate its redefinition over a period of time, a paradox which may repeat itself many times as the activity changes, develops or fades out.

Maximal participation of service users and carers throughout the process

All too often, schemes and projects are conjured up by professionals, money is found, staff time is allocated, proposals are worked out in detail, before anyone thinks of consulting the people who are meant to be central – the service users themselves. The rhetoric of the development of empowerment needs to be reflected throughout the reality of the process of empowering people.

There is thus a need to avoid professionals dictating the agenda of activity, and this implies living with the risk of a lack of consumer leadership by service users. Inherently, social workers occupy strategic positions in relation to their legal obligations and to their organisational base. Empowerment-in-practice necessitates a careful handling of the process of development itself. It is all too easy for professionals to misuse their undoubted structural power and damage initiatives, possible irretrievably.

Empowering work invariably should be paced by the service user/carer

Central to the process is the principle that the social worker as the professional does not impose the process of empowerment on a person. Individuals may be given the option of taking part. Once involved, they should have control over the process: the pace of the activity should be determined by the service user and/or carer and not by the social worker.

Setting a long enough time scale

It is important to recognise that the process of empowering people takes time. In the US, where empowerment-oriented self-help programmes have been running for many years, a Director of Save the Children Fund described to the author the typical time scale for the process of shifting from initial facilitation by professionals to autonomous activity, as ten to twelve years.

Given that the empowering process is slow, there is a need to develop a network of contacts in one area, overcome people's lack of willingess to confide in officials, build up trust and avoid being discriminating or patronising towards people. Individuals or groups such as carers' groups seeking advice or information may prefer to get support from a professional, rather than to seek it from a friend or neighbour who then would know things about them they would rather keep private.

Professionals should help their agencies learn from experience

To the extent that the development of a user-led or self-help project leads to novel and perhaps instructive ways of approaching a task or service, there should be ways of feeding in this experience constructively to the social work agency itself. For example, in the Humberside Project, management in both voluntary agency and social services could have examined usefully the learning derived in the project from staff working as a 'flat team' without a recognised project leader. How would such experience translate, for example, into the running of a day centre or a residential home?

Values

A colleague responded to a question about why he had not joined users in protesting about cuts in services, including grants to self-help and carers' groups: 'It wouldn't do any good. The decision has already been made, and once made, you have to make the best of it.' This is a view from a disempowered standpoint. It is preferable to carry out empowerment-in-practice from a value position which informs positive assertion of values which challenge oppression, of whatever kind.

Anti-oppressiveness

It is axiomatic that empowerment-in-practice should be rooted in anti-oppressive values. There is a need for anti-oppressive practice to permeate all domains of practice. The dialogic nature of work with service users and carers suggests an interactive process of continually revisiting values and re-negotiating them, rather than simply imposing them as a take-it-or-leave-it imposition by professionals.

A political activity

Inevitably, progress towards empowerment involves taking a political stance which is critical of the status quo. Empowering social work is inherently a political activity. In the latter part of the twentieth century, the words 'self-help' conjure up government cutbacks and people being expected to self-care, that is cope with their problems with minimal resources and support from social workers and the State. The map of social work services has been redrawn since the NHS and

Community Care Act 1990, so as to reflect an enhanced emphasis on market competition, private provision and the voluntary sector. Whilst self-help can be presented as a politically neutral concept, the contemporary social and political context makes it possible to use it to accelerate the trends just described. Or, it can offer a way of challenging them.

Just because we might agree with Gladstone (1979) that a large-scale shift of resource allocation away from statutory to voluntary organisations is desirable, this is no guarantee that all the criticisms we make of the bureaucratic approach of service delivery by professionals will be no longer valid. On the contrary, the problem is social and political rather than economic, in that our values need to change so as to view the service users of services as able to play an empowered, that is, a more active and powerful part in service delivery. The balance of power between helpers and helped, professionals and service users, needs to be shifted in favour of people helped and service users. The current tendency for community care to develop very unevenly throughout the country and for great unfairness to accompany the stratifications of informal care to the disadvantage of women and those in the lower social classes (Ungerson, 1987, p. 153), highlights the danger of self-help and mutual care becoming part of the bleak outlook for isolated, depressed and unsupported carers.

Participation rather than consumerism

The internal markets created by legislation such as the NHS and Community Care Act 1990 have the effect of legitimating concepts, principles and practices which are capable of more than one interpretation. Thus, the principles of partnership and empowerment can be implemented from a consumerist point of view, thereby giving the service user greater choice as a consumer of social services. But they can also be viewed from a participative perspective, as requiring the democratisation of services and the empowerment of service users.

Mutual aid rather than individualism

In addressing the task of relating social work to self-help, self-care and user-led practice, in the resource-constrained circumstances referred to, we have to remind ourselves of the rationale for encouraging self-help. It is not the emphasis on individuals pulling themselves up by their own bootstraps which appeals, but rather the centrality of mutual aid in an environment where all are encouraged to participate irrespective of their social or professional position. This provides a means of transcending the consumerist approach to providing community care, for example. The most important purpose of self-help is thus not helping smaller social work organisations become more cost-effective but enabling people to live a better quality life in a better society. Self-help as described in the preceding chapters points to means by which people can have a greater say in the nature and delivery of their services, either independently of, enabled by, or in partnership with, social workers. Mutual aid must be emphasised in the present social and economic climate, partly as an antidote to rampant individualism and consumerism.

Professional non-professionalism and anti-professional professionalism

The divisions between different categories and levels of empowering activity bring one aspect potentially into conflict with another. One person's empowerment may be another person's disempowerment. Professionals may be empowered at the expense of managers or service users. Self-help therapy and community action may conflict; careful work may be needed to reconcile therapy with self-advocacy. Paradox is threaded through the whole enterprise, as indeed it is inherent in the notion of non-professional service users developing an expertise in self-help which may be regarded as professional, while professionals cultivate what Parsloe referred to earlier as anti-professionalism!

Developing practice beyond a 'Western' middle-class agenda

The inclusion of the Nijeri Kori initiative in Chapter 4 redresses to a small extent the inherent ethnocentrism and Western elitism of the social work literature, as well as keeping on the agenda the need to view critically our dependence on the experience of white middle-class academia in the US, which is a feature of literature in the field of self-help groups, for example. It also highlights the lessons we can learn from what are called Third World settings, where people often live in conditions of great political difficulty, social uncertainty and physical want. Is empowering people more of an achievement in Britain or among poor people of Bangladesh?

It may be argued that empowerment will be more imaginatively and constructively employed in a social context where people are highly motivated towards, involved in, and optimistic about, grassroots politics and community action. Before undertaking new work, it will be necessary for social workers to assess local conditions in terms of the potential viability of developing an empowered practice and decide how to implement it in the different domains referred to in the framework set out in Chapter 2.

Empowerment as a challenge to professional power and inequalities

Developments in such areas as anti-oppressive practice and self-advocacy, heighten the need to take seriously the efforts of people who have been on the receiving end of inadequate services to improve their self-care and services as well! A good illustration of how to carry forward such principles is provided by the publication by David and Althea Brandon (1988) in the area of normalisation, emphasising that a shared goal should be assuring everybody, irrespective of their circumstances, the expectation of an ordinary way of living. A radical challenge to the structural power of the professional comes from the groups such as Survivors Speak Out, who challenge

professional rhetoric about patient participation and consultation with clients.

   This is closely allied with the notion of social workers and
service users treating each other as equals. There is a need to
promote more real and effective sharing and co-operation
between service users and professionals. In the process, as was
noted by the (then) DHSS funded self-help project in Britain
(Fielding, 1989, p. 7), there is a need for social workers to
learn how to be both reactive and proactive. The proactive
role is a necessity also for service users and carers to initiate
mutual aid and self-care partnerships and networks.

Policies

Widening the variety and scope of social work roles

Despite their finding that self-help has little formal impact,
Knight and Hayes recommend that it should be a key feature of
policies to revitalise the inner cities (Knight and Hayes, 1981,
p. 95), since with the right policies and resources it could be
very effective. Prominent policy priorities should include a positive commitment by politicians and managers to ensuring that
co-ordination between professionals and service users works effectively. Social workers should be involved at the interface between service users and these different levels. This is a
demanding responsibility complicated by multiple contracting
of service provision, involving statutory, voluntary, private and
informal sectors. It involves addressing people's needs *with*
them, confirming and developing their independence, acknowledging and demonstrating the power they have already, rather
than presuming it is for professional workers to empower them.

Enhancing the levels of social work practice

A further reason for social workers taking a wider perspective
is to ensure that, where appropriate, a continuum of activity

is encouraged, so that individual effort is not isolated from groups and the community dimension has the opportunity to influence individuals and groups. Thus, social work, for example, has a role to play in the training, support and re-sourcing of a range of professionals, volunteers, carers and service users, working in neighbourhoods alongside profes-sional workers in social work and social care. The community care plans of local authorities could provide a basis for a broader-based neighbourhood-wide perception by people in the statutory, voluntary, private and informal sectors of a wider range of human needs and responses to them by those working in the human services. We should bear in mind the following themes:

- The need for development to avoid professionals exploit-ing rather than empowering service users
- The need to avoid professionals taking over activities
- The need to enable service users and carers to assess what services they need
- The need to enable service users to manage the delivery of necessary resources
- The need to enable service users to evaluate services.

Focusing on undervalued and marginalised issues

There is little doubt that the field of self-help flourishes in, among other things, areas neglected, marginalised, scorned, ignored and undervalued by professionals. This is not ac-cidental. Social workers should appreciate this strength of the self-help field and encourage it accordingly, since much of work of social workers falls into the above category.

But the task of doing something about this is not straight-forward. Two issues which arise concern the way which social workers may promote specialist work with, say, an Asian group and the consequences of that initiative for the situa-tion of Asian people in relation to the nature and quality of their lives. We can see the argument clearly in relation to their lives. We can see the argument clearly in relation to decisions, taken in the light of funding under Section 11 of the Local Government Act 1966, to employ a black worker, specifically to work on Black issues. This is how a black worker involved in such an initiative in the late 1980s put it, in an interview for this book (. . . indicates long pause; . . short pause; [. . .] omitted words):

> many black people are employed in temporary schemes or pro-jects on low wages . . . agencies may have obtained funds through such sources as Section 11 of the Local Government Act (1966) . . . agencies may allocate to black or disabled people a quota for a reservation of places in the work force . . . quota or reservation policies have the advantage for agencies that they in-crease the profile of their work with undervalued groups in the community . . . but three criticisms can be made . . . first there is often no permanence about the situation of such workers . . . sec-ond tensions between those moving into reserved posts and other workers and those denied employment may have unpleasant con-sequences . . . third such policies are unfair in principle because they fill gaps in the labour market without actually increasing overall access to the labour market for the people concerned . . . the way Section 11 is actually employed and used by the local authority . . the gains are all on the side of the local authority and the losses are on the side of the workers . . . the community gains but it is a very short-term gain and it is a very uncertain vulnerable gain [. . .] black people are employed to work with black people. All the white colleagues usually offload the work . . . they are seen as specialist and they are specialist in one sense, that they do bring particular skills that social services does lack . . but then they are expected to do the work with the black community . . . quite often in my experience they are expected to do much higher level work than their colleagues would do . . . they are seen as the answer to all the white issues and represent the entire black community . . but at the same time they are in a very vulner-able position which the statutory agency doesn't recognise be-cause they have to tread a very thin line between the community's expectation and what the community sees of them and what the statutory body want them to do . . . and because they are on Sec-

tion 11 funding it is by definition discriminatory . . . there are no two ways about it because they are on completely different terms and conditions and contract of employment and monetarily . . . than their white colleagues in mainstream employment [. . .] on the service delivery side of it . . the fact is that because black issues are marginalised . . it's not seen as an integral part of the work . . . there's the work and then the black issues are attached to it and if say . . for example . . the black funding was actually withdrawn from the black workers then by definition the black workers would be withdrawn . . . because that's the link . . . black workers can exist outside the structure and the community exists outside the structure and I think it's a very dangerous position to get into and therefore I think that it is very important that the work . . the issues are integrated . . . not the people [. . .] In a statutory set-up the only way that you would secure the long-term guarantee that the community is actually served is through integrating the issues . . . and also I think that all the statutory workers should be given an absolutely categorical guarantee on their work contract . . that if their funding is withdrawn that they will be taken on mainstream funding . . . because if the council is serious about the fact that the black work is their priority and it is the income that's important to them . . then you've got to give them the guarantee and if you give them the guarantee they can ensure that people themselves don't feel vulnerable in their jobs and that there is the long-term possibility of securing service to the community . . because otherwise you are in constant fear of your funding being withdrawn and you know that the minute you go . . after that there's not going to be any work done . . because it's the way the system works and the only way you can mitigate it is by positive steps. (Interview with member of Asian Self-help Group)

The above extract, despite legislative changes since then, illustrates both particular features of the situation of black people and also general aspects of, and general issues in relation to, empowering workers and service users, applicable just as strongly in the contract culture of the 1990s as it was in the late 1980s. Three things come across clearly: the poor bargaining position of black people, the vulnerability of their

situation and their work, and the tendency for crude positive discrimination to emphasise their marginalisation as individual groups. Rather, empowerment should be part of a
policy of positive action in respect of discriminated-against
people.

Resources

It is necessary to conclude this book with a re-emphasis of the
issue of resources. It is the acid test of the commitment of
professionals to self-help and user-led initiatives. In 1989 the
Department of Health-sponsored £1.75m initiative ended, involving eighteen self-help projects in different parts of England. What long-term implications for the field of self-help
does this 'pump-priming' approach to development have?
What responsibility should be taken by the government and
other agencies and organisations for the continued support
of such activities? Clearly, pump priming is no way to ensure
a continued flow of funding for a project or activity. Knight
and Hayes (1981, p. 95) point out that insufficient funds and
lack of suitable premises are key constraints on the effectiveness of self-help groups. Professionals have a role to play in
ensuring that empowering work is not stifled or impeded
through such factors. The next stage is for professionals to
recognise that they have a responsibility to phase themselves
out of the picture: integral programmes perhaps should be
working towards facilitation and facilitated ones towards autonomy. It is questionable whether increased resources alone
can improve the circumstances of people, since often it is the
professionals who benefit most from special programmes and
projects (Knight and Hayes, 1981, p. 96). This leads to the
conclusion that to ensure maximum effectiveness, resources
should be given to people who need them, with a minimum
of facilitators. 'This suggests giving money to inner city residents who would be responsible for its proper use, in many
cases this would involve employing local people as *indigenous*

workers' (Knight and Hayes, 1981, p. 96, emphasis in original).

Much of what we have argued at length above rests on different aspects of the simple but fundamental issue of *power*, chief among which are the power of the service user to choose and the extent to which any redistribution of power between professionals and service users is conceivable in practice.

The power to choose

Regarding the first of these, the power to choose, advice services provide an instructive alternative to the service delivery approach. In the study conducted by Knight and Hayes of thirty self-help community groups, they suggest the reason for a high level of user satisfaction may be because service users can take the initiative and can take or leave the advice (Knight and Hayes, 1981, p. 94). This gives us a clue to an important principle inherent in effective self-help: namely ensuring that service users of social work services retain a maximum degree of control over the extent to which they receive services. It is not only the right to decide whether to receive services which is important to service users, but also the need to prioritise empowering them at least on a par with the rationing of resources (Darvill and Smale, 1990, p. 5). Over and above this, there is a case for providing service users with the means to meet their own needs, rather than processing their situations through professional assessment, care planning and implementation (Smale, Tuson, Biehal, and Marsh, 1993).

The redistribution of resources

As far as the redistribution of power between social workers and service users is concerned, clearly there are some areas where it will never happen, many where it is extremely unlikely and perhaps only a few where it will be considered as possible and potentially beneficial to the interests of both parties. Translating this into resource terms, we are talking about holding the existing allocation of resources in real terms and increasing it in proportion to discovered need. Where appropriate, this means not cancelling any resources removed from the professional area but transferring them to user-led initiatives where possible.

Having said that, we need to stand back behind the resources question and set it in a broader context. Chapter 2 offers a framework within which empowering work can be undertaken. This implies:

- minimising service users' dependence on professional workers
- looking critically at how social workers relate to user-led initiatives
- increasingly making use of groups and network approaches to work with volunteers, relatives, carers, friends, neighbours, many organisations and agencies in and out of social work as well as with the local media
- not simply mobilising fresh initiatives, but tapping into what already exists in the community
- trying to create in oneself and in others a better understanding of the relationship between the helping acts of professionals and the helping and self-helping mechanisms which are already part of everyday life.

This is an area in which there is unlikely to be a sudden enlightenments, a fanfare of trumpets and a once-and-for-all solution. On the contrary, as in so much really useful social work, the slow and at times painful path to better practice is what counts.

Self-empowerment and the empowerment of practice

The most cogent argument for the development of empowering and productive relationships between service users and social workers arises from the case made in this book, for the empowerment of social workers and, even more, for the empowerment of service users themselves, in furtherance of the wider aim of empowering others in the community. For the paradigm of empowerment to have real benefits for service users, practitioners, managers, organisations and communities, its significance for the redistribution of power at all levels and in all sectors of society needs to be taken seriously, rather than located, or rather constrained, within the dominant ideology of consumerism. Fundamentally, the paradigm of empowerment is, and should remain, dangerous and challenging to powerful people: politicians, managers and practitioners. The challenge of empowerment-in-practice is to develop a truly anti-oppressive theory in and through reflective practice.

Bibliography

Abramovitz, Mimi (1987) 'Making Gender a Variable in Social Work Teaching', *Journal of Teaching in Social Work*, vol. 1, no. 1, pp. 29–52.

Adams, Robert (1976) 'Intermediate Treatment: Looking at Some Patterns of Intervention', *Youth Social Work Bulletin*, vol. 3, no. 2 (February-March) pp. 9–12.

Adams, Robert *et al.* (eds) (1981) *A Measure of Diversion? Case Studies in Intermediate Treatment* Leicester, National Youth Bureau.

Adams, Robert (1989) 'Parents, Children under Five and Empowerment in the Humberside Project', Humberside College of Higher Education.

Adams, Robert (1991) *Protests by Pupils: Empowerment, Schooling and the State*, Basingstoke, Falmer.

Adams, Robert (1992) *Empowering Clients* (video in Social Work Theories series) Brighton, Pavilion.

Adams, Robert (1994) *Prison Riots in Britain and the USA*, 2nd edn, London, Macmillan.

Adams, Robert (forthcoming) *Quality Social Work*, London, Macmillan.

Adams, Robert (forthcoming) *The Personal Social Services: Clients, Consumers or Citizens?*, Harlow, Longman.

Adams, Robert and Lindenfield, Gael (1985) *Self-Help and Mental Health*, Ilkley, Self-Help Associates.

Agel, Jeremy (1971) *Radical Therapist: The Radical Therapist Collective*, New York, Ballantine Books.

Altman, Dennis (1986) *AIDS and the New Puritanism*, London, Pluto Press.

Arnstein, S. (1969) 'A Ladder of Citizen Participation', *Journal of the American Institute of Planners*, vol. 35, no. 4, pp. 216–22.

Asian Resource Centre (1987) *Annual Report 1986–87*, Birmingham, Asian Resource Centre.

Audit Commission for Local Authorities in England and Wales (1986) *Making a Reality of Community Care*, A Report by the Audit Commission, London, HMSO.

Aves, G. (1969) *The Voluntary Worker in the Social Services*, London, Allen & Unwin.

Back, Kurt W. (1972) *Beyond Words: The Story of Sensitivity Training and the Encounter Movement*, New York, Russell Sage.

Bagguley, P. (1991) *From Protest to Acquiescence: Political Movements of the Unemployed*, London, Macmillan.

Baistow, Karen (1994) 'Liberation and Regulation? Some Paradoxes of Empowerment', *Critical Social Policy*, issue 42, vol. 14, no. 3 (Winter 1994–5) pp. 34–46.

Bakker, Bert and Karel, Mattieu (1983) 'Self-Help: Wolf or Lamb?', in Pancoast *et al.* pp. 159–81.

Balloch, Susan *et al.* (1985) *Caring for Unemployed People*, London, Bedford Square/NCVO.

Bamford, Terry (1982) *Managing Social Work*, London, Tavistock.

Bankoff, Elizabeth A. (1979) 'Widow Groups as an Alternative to Informal Social Support', in Lieberman *et al.* (1979) pp. 181–93.

Barber, James G. (1991) *Beyond Casework*, BASW/Macmillan, London.

Barclay Report (1982) See Social Work, National Institute for (1982).

BASW (1980) 'Skills for Social Workers in the 1980s', Birmingham, BASW.

BASW (1984) 'Social Work in the Community', Birmingham, BASW (January 1984).

Bell, L. (1989) 'Is Psychotherapy More Empowering to the Therapist than the Client?', *Clinical Psychology Forum*, vol. 23, pp. 12–14.

Beresford, Peter (undated) 'Patch in Perspective: Decentralising and Democratising Social Services', London, Battersea Community Action.

Beresford, Peter and Croft, Suzy (1981) 'Community Control of Social Services Departments', London, Battersea Community Action.

Beresford, P. and Croft, S. (1986) *Whose Welfare: Private Care or Public Services?*, Brighton, Lewis Cohen Urban Studies.

Beresford, P. and Croft, S. (1993) *Citizen Involvement: A Practical Guide for Change*, London, BASW/Macmillan.

Birchall, Johnston (1988) *Building Communities the Co-operative Way*, London, Routledge & Kegan Paul.

Boateng, Paul (1986) 'Society and Crisis, 1984 and Beyond', in BASW (1986) pp. 3–6.

Bond, Gary *et al.* (1979) 'Growth of a Medical Self-Help Group', in Lieberman *et al.* (1979) pp. 43–66.

Bond, Gary and Reibstein, Janet (1979) 'Changing Goals in Women's Consciousness-Raising', in Lieberman *et al.* (1979) pp. 95–115.

Borman, Leonard D. (1979) 'Characteristics of Development and Growth', in Liberman *et al.* (1979) pp. 13–42.

Borman, Leonard D. (1982) 'Helping People to Help Themselves: Self-Help and Prevention', *Prevention in Human Services*, vol. 1, no. 3 (Spring).

Brankaerts, Jan (1983) 'Birth of the Movement: Early Milestones', in Pancoast *et al.* (1983) pp. 143–58.

Brandon, David and Brandon, Althea (1988) *Putting People First: A Handbook in the Practical Application of Ordinary Living Principles*, London, Good Impressions.

Braye, Suzy and Preston-Shoot, Michael (1995) *Empowering Practice in Social Care*, Buckingham, Open University.

Brodsky, Annette M. (1981) 'The Consciousness-Raising Group as a Model for Therapy with Women', in Howell and Bayes (1981) pp. 572–80.

Caplan, Gerald and Killilea, Marie (1976) *Support Systems and Mutual Help: Multi-disciplinary Explorations*, New York, Grune & Stratton.

CCETSW (1991) *Rules and Requirements for the Diploma in Social Work* (Paper 30) London, CCETSW.

Chamberlain, Mary (1981) *Old Wives' Tales*, London, Virago.

Clarke, Michael and Stewart, John (1992) *Citizens and Local Democracy: Empowerment: a Theme for the 1990s*, Luton, Local Government Management Board.

Coulshed, V. (1991) *Social Work Practice: An Introduction*, London, BASW/Macmillan.

Craig, Gary (1989) 'Community Work and the State', *Community Development Journal*, vol. 24, no. 1, pp. 3–18.

Craig, Gary (1992) *Cash or Care: A Question of Choice?*, Social Policy Research Unit, York, University of York.

Croft, Gerry, Lawson, Brian, and Smith, Ian (1990) 'The Development of Community Social Work in Airedale, Castleford 1980–1987', in Giles, Darvill and Gerald Smale (eds), *Partners in Empowerment: Networks of Innovation in Social Work*, London, National Institute for Social Work, pp. 133–50.

Croft, Suzy and Beresford, Peter (1989) 'User-Involvement, Citizenship and Social Policy', *Critical Social Policy*, issue 26, vol. 9, no. 2 (Autumn) pp. 5–18.

Culley, Margo and Portuges Catherine, (eds) (1985) *Gendered Subjects: the Dynamics of Feminist Teaching*, London, Routledge & Kegan Paul.

Cunningham, Ian. (1994) 'Interactive Holistic Research: Researching Self-Managed Learning', in Reason (ed.) (1994) pp. 163–81.

Darvill, Giles and Munday, Brian (1984) *Volunteers in the Personal Social Services*, London, Tavistock.

Darvill, Giles and Smale, Gerald (eds) (1990) *Partners in Empowerment: Networks of Innovation in Social Work*, London, NISW.

Darvill, Giles and Munday, Brian (1984) *Volunteers in the Personal Social Services*, London, Tavistock.

Dingwall, R. (1988) 'Empowerment or Enforcement: Some Questions About Power and Control in Divorce mediation?', in R. Dingwall and John M. Eckelaar (eds), *Divorce Mediation and the Legal Process*, Oxford, Clarendon Press.

Donnan, Linda and Lenton, Sue (1985) *Helping Ourselves: A Handbook for Women Starting Groups*, Toronto, Women's Press.

Dumont, Matther P. (1971) *The Absurd Healer: Perspectives of a Community Psychiatrist*, New York, Viking Press.

Dumont, Matthew P. (1972) 'Revenue Sharing and the Unbuilding of Pyramids', *American Journal of Orthopsychiatry*, vol. 42, no. 2 (March) pp. 219–31.

Dutt, R. (1989) 'Griffiths Really Is a White Paper', *Social Work Today*, 1 March, pp. 16–17.

Evans, Liz *et al.* (1986) *Working with Parents of Handicapped Children*, London, Bedford Square/NCVO.

Ferrand-Bechman, Dan (1983) 'Voluntary Action in the Welfare State', in Pancoast *et al.* (1983) pp. 183–201.

Fielding, Nick (1989) 'No More Help for Self-Helpers', *Community Care*, 755 (23 March) p. 7.

Fosterling, F. (1985) 'Attributional Retraining: A Review', *Psychological Bulletin*, 98, pp. 495–512.

Franklin, B. (1986) *The Rights of Children*, Oxford, Blackwell.

Freire, Paulo (1972) (reprinted 1986) *Pedagogy of the Oppressed*, Harmondsworth, Penguin.

Furlong, Mark (1987) 'A Rationale for the Use of Empowerment as a Goal in Casework', *Australian Social Work*, vol. 40, no. 3 pp. 25–30.

Gartner, Alan and Riessman, Frank (1977) *Self-Help in the Human Services*, London, Jossey-Bass.

Gartner, Alan and Riessman, Frank (1984) *The Self-Help Revolution*, New York, Human Sciences Press.

Gawlinski, George and Graessle, Lois (1988) *Planning Together: The Art of Effective Teamwork*, London, Bedford Square/NCVO.

Gibson, Tony (1979) *People Power: Communities and Work Groups in Action*, Harmondsworth, Penguin.

Gill, Martin and Andrews, Margaret (1987) 'Volunteers: Result Finds Volunteer Use Receives Little Priority During Training', *Social Work Today* (11 May)

Goldberg, E.M. (1966) *Welfare in the Community: Talks on Social Work to Welfare Officers*, London, Bedford Square.

Green, David (1991) *Empowering the Parents: How to Break the Schools Monopoly*, London, Inner London Education Authority Health and Welfare Unit.

Griffiths, Kate (1991) *Consulting with Chinese Communities*, London, King, Feel Centre.

Griffiths, Roy (1988) *Community Care: Agenda for Action: A Report on the Secretary of State for Social Services*, London, HMSO.

Hadley, Roger and McGrath, Morag (1981) *Going Local: Neighbourhood Social Services*, London, NCVO.

Hadley, Roger and Hatch, Stephen (1981) *Social Welfare and the Failure of the State: Centralised Social Services and Participating Alternatives*, London, Allen & Unwin.

Hadley, Roger, Dale, Peter and Sills, Patrick (1984) *Decentralising Social Services: A Model for Change*, London, NCVO.

Hadley, Roger and McGrath, Morag (1980) *Going Local: Neighbourhood Social Services*, London, NCVO.

Hadley, Roger *et al.* (1987) *A Community Worker's Handbook*, London, Tavistock.

Hallowitz, Emmanuel and Riessman, Frank (1967) 'The Role of the Indigenous Non-Professional in a Community Mental Health Neighbourhood', *American Journal of Orthopsychiatry*, 37, pp. 766–78.

Hatch, Stephen and Kickbusch, Ilona (eds) (1983) *Self-Help and Health in Europe: New Approaches in Health Care*, Copenhagen, World Health Organisation, Registered Office for Europe.

Haug, Maire and Sussman, Marvin B. (1969) 'Professional Autonomy and the Revolt of the Client', *Social Problems*, 17, pp. 153–61.

Henderson, P. and Thomas, D. (1980) *Skills in Neighbourhood Work*, London, Allen & Unwin.

Heron, John (1990) *Helping the Client: A Creative Practical Guide*, London, Sage.

Hirst, Paul (1994) *Associative Democracy: New Forms of Economic and Social Governance*, Oxford, Polity Press.

Holdsworth, Lisa (1991) *Empowerment: Social Work with Physically Disabled People*, Social Work Monographs, No. 97, University of East Anglia, Norwich.

Holloway, Christine and Otto, Shirley (1986) *Getting Organised: A Handbook for Non-Statutory Organisations*, London, Bedford Square/NCVO.

Holme, Anthea and Maizels, Joan (1978) *Social Workers and Volunteers*, London, Allen & Unwin.

hooks, bell (1989) *Thinking Feminist: Talking Black*, London, Sheba.

hooks, bell (1991) *Yearning: Race, Gender and Cultural Politics*, London, Turnaround Press.

Howell, Elizabeth (1981) *Psychotherapy with Women Clients: the Impact of Feminism*, in Howell and Bayes (eds) *Women and Mental Health*, Basic Books, New York, pp. 509–13.

Howell, Elizabeth and Bayes, Marjorie (1981) *Women and Mental Health*, New York, Basic Books.

Hulke, Malcolm (ed.) (1978) *The Encyclopædia of Alternative Medicine and Self-Help*, London, Rider & Co.

Hurvitz, Nathan (1970) 'Peer Self-Help Therapy Groups and their Implications for Psychotherapy', *Psychotherapy, Research and Practice*, vol. 7, no. 10 (Spring) pp. 41–9.

Hurvitz, Nathan (1974) 'Peer Self-Help Psychotherapy Groups: Psychotherapy without Psychotherapists', in Roman and Trice (1974) pp. 84–137.

Jacobs, Sidney and Popple, Keith (eds) (1994) *Community Work in the 1990s*, Nottingham, Spokesman.

Jones, S. (1981) *Working Together: Partnerships in Local Social Services: A Working Party Report*, London, Bedford Square/NCVO.

Katz, Alfred H. (1970) 'Self-Help Organisations and Volunteer Participation in Social Welfare', *Social Work*, 15 (January) pp. 51–60.

Katz, Alfred H. and Bender, Eugene I. (1976) *The Strength in Us: Self-Help Groups in the Modern World*, New Viewpoints, New York, Franklin Watts.

Key, Michael, Hudson, Peter and Armstrong, John (1976) *Evaluation Theory and Community Work*, London, Young Volunteer Force Foundation.

Killilea, Marie (1976) 'Mutual Help Organisations: Interpretations in the Literature', in Caplan and Killilea (1976) pp. 37–87.

Kleiman, M. A. *et al.* (1976) 'Collaboration and Its Discontents: The Perils of Partnership', *Journal of Applied Behavioural Science*, 12, Part 3, pp. 403–10.

Knight, Barry and Hayes, Ruth (1981) *Self-Help in the Inner City*, London, London Voluntary Service Council.

Knowles, M. (1984) *The Adult Learner: A Neglected Species*, Houston, USA, Gulf Publishing.

Kropotkin, P. (1902) *Mutual Aid: A Factor in Evolution*, Boston, Porter Sargeant.

Kuhn, Thomas S. (1970) *The Structure of Scientific Revolutions*, 2nd edn, Chicago, University of Chicago Press.

Kurowska, Shiela (1984) *Employing People in Voluntary Organisations*, London, Bedford Square/NVCO.

Laslett, Peter (1983) *The World We Have Lost – Further Explored*, London, Methuen.

Lawson, M. (1991) 'A Recipient's View', in S. Ramon (ed.), *Beyond Community Care: Normalisation and Integration Work*, London, MIND/Macmillan, pp. 62–83.

Leiberman, Morton *et al.* (1979) 'Effectiveness of Women's Consciousness Raising', in Lieberman *et al.* (1979) pp. 341–61.

Lerner, M.P. (1979) 'Surplus Powerlessness', *Social Policy*, Jan/Feb, pp. 19–27.

Levy, Laureen *et al.* (1986) *Finding Our Own Solutions: Women's Experience of Mental Health Care*, London, MIND.

Lieberman, Morton, Solow, Nancy, Bond, Gary R. and Reibstein, Janet (1981) 'The Psychotherapeutic Impact of Women's Consciousness-Raising', in Howell and Bayes (1981), pp. 531–99.

Levy, Leon H. (1976) 'Self-Help Groups: Types and Psychological Processes', *Journal of Applied Behavioural Science, 12, part 3, pp. 310–22.*

Levy, Leon H. (1978) 'Self-Help Groups Viewed by Mental Health Professionals', *Journal of Applied Behavioural Science*, 12, Part 3, pp. 310–22.

Levy, Leon H. (1979) 'Processes and Activities in Groups' in Lieberman *et al.* (1979) pp. 234–71.

Levy, Leo (1982) 'Mutual Support Groups in Great Britain', *Social Service in Medicine*, 16(13), pp. 1265–75.

Lieberman, Morton A. and Bond, Gary R. (1978) 'Self-Help: Problems of Measuring Outcomes', *Small Group Behaviour*, vol. 9, no. 2 (May) pp. 221–41.

Lieberman, Morton (1979) 'Analysing Change Mechanisms in Groups', in Lieberman *et al.* (1979) pp. 194–233.

Lieberman, Morton and Borman, Leonard D. (1976) 'Self-Help and Social Research', *Journal of Applied Behavioural Science*, 12, Part 3, pp. 455–63.

Lieberman, Morton *et al.* (1979) *Self-Help Groups for Coping with Crisis Origins. Members, Processes and Impact*, San Francisco, Jossey-Bass.

Lindenfield, Gael (1986) *Assert Yourself*, Ilkley, Self-Help Associates.

Lindenfield, Gael and Adams, Robert (1984) *Problem Solving Through Self-Help Groups*, Ilkley, Self-Help Associates.

Living Options in Practice, 1992, *Project Paper No. 3, Achieving User Participation*, London, King's Fund Centre.

Longres, J. F. and McLeod, E. (1980) 'Consciousness Raising and Social Work Practice', *Social Casework*, May, pp. 267–76.

Lurie, Harry (ed.) (1965) *Encyclopædia of Social Work*, National Association of Social Workers.

Marieskind, Helen I. (1984) 'Women's Self-Help Groups', in Gartner and Riessman (1984) pp. 27–32.

McLeod, Eileen (1987) 'Some Lessons from Teaching Feminist Social Work', *Social Work Education*, vol. 7, no. 1, pp. 29–37.

Mezirow, Jack (1983) 'A Critical Theory of Adult Learning and Education', in Malcolm Tight (ed.), *Adult Learning and Education*, Beckenham, Kent, Croom Helm, pp. 124–38.

Moeller, Michael L. (1983) *The New Group Therapy*, Princeton, Van Nostrand.

Mowrer, O. Hobart (1972) 'Integrity Groups: Principles and Procedures', *The Counselling Psychologist*, 3, pp. 7–33.

Mowrer, O. Hobart (1984) 'The Mental Health Professions and Mutual Help Programs: Co-optation or Collaboration?', in Gartner and Riessman (1984) pp. 139–54.

Mullender, A. and Ward, D. (1988) 'What is Practice-Led Research into Groupwork?', in P. Wedge (ed.), *Social Work – A Third Look at Research into Practice: Proceedings of the Third Annual JUC/BASW Conference, London, September 1987*, Birmingham, BASW.

Mullender, Audrey and Ward, Dave (1991) *Self-Directed Groupwork: Users Take Action for Empowerment*, London, Whiting & Birch.

Norman, Janet (1976) 'Consciousness-Raising: Self-Help in the Women's Movement', in Katz and Bender (1976), chapter 16.

Ohri, A. Manning, B. and Curno, P. (eds) (1982) *Community Work and Racism*, London, ACW/Routledge.

O'Sullivan, Terence (1994) 'Why Don't Social Workers Work in Partnership With People?', unpublished paper, University of Humberside, Hull.

Page, R. (1992) 'Empowerment, Oppression and Beyond: A Coherent Strategy? A Reply to Ward and Mullender', *Critical Social Policy*, issue 35, Autumn, pp. 89–92.

Pancoast, Diane L., Parker, Paul and Forland, Charles (1983) *Rediscovering Self-Help: Its Role in Social Care*, Beverly Hills, Sage.

Parsloe, Phyllida (1986) 'What Skills do Social Workers Need?', in BASW (1986) pp. 7–15.

Patton, Michael Quinn (1982) *Practical Evaluation*, Beverly Hills, Sage.

Payne, Malcolm (1991) *Modern Social Work Theory: A Critical Introduction*, London, Macmillan.

Phillipson, C. (1989) 'Challenging Dependency: Towards a New Social Work With Older People', in M. Langan, and P. Lee (eds), *Radical Social Work Today*, London, Unwin Hyman, pp. 192–207.

Phillipson, Julia (1992) *Practising Equality: Women, Men and Social Work*, Improving Social Work Education and Training, No. 10, CCETSW, London.

Preston-Shoot, Michael (1987) *Effective Groupwork*, London, BASW/Macmillan.

Rappaport, J. (1984) 'Studies in Empowerment: Introduction to the Issue', *Prevention in Human Services*, vol. 3, nos 2/3, pp. 1–7.

Reason, P. (ed.) (1994) *Human Inquiry in Action: Developments in New Paradigm Research*, London, Sage.

Reason, P. and Rowan, J. (eds) (1981) *Human Inquiry: A Sourcebook of New Paradigm Research*, Chichester, John Wiley.

Richardson, Ann (1983) 'English Self-Help: Varied Patterns and Practices', in Pancoast *et al.* (1983) pp. 203–21.

Richardson, Ann (1984) *Working with Self-Help Groups: A Guide for Local Professionals*, London, Bedford Square/NCVO.

Richardson, Ann and Goodman, Meg (1983) *Self-Help and Social Care: Mutual Aid Organisations in Practice*, London, Policy Studies Institute.

Riessman, Frank (1965) 'The "Helper" Therapy Principle', *Social Work*, 10 (April).

Robinson, David and Henry, Stuart (1977) *Self-Help and Health: Mutual Aid for Modern Problems*, New York, Jason Aronson.

Rojek, Chris (1986) 'The "Subject" in Social Work', *British Journal of Social Work*, vol. 16, no. 1, pp. 65–79.

Roman, Paul M. and Trice, Harrison M. (1974) *The Sociology of Psychotherapy*, New York, Jason Aronson.

Rowbothom, Shelia *et al.* (1980) *Beyond the Fragments, Feminism and the Making of Socialism*, London, Merlin.

Russel-Erlich, John and Rivera, Felix G. (1986) 'Community Empowerment as a Non-Problem', *Journal of Sociology and Social Welfare*, vol. 13, no. 3, pp. 451–65.

Rutherford, J. (ed.), (1990) *Identity: Community, Culture, Difference*, London, Lawrence & Wishart.

Sainsbury, Eric (1989), 'Participation and Paternalism', in Steven Shardlow (ed.), *The Values of Change in Social Work*, London, Tavistock/Routledge, pp. 98–113.

Salaman, Graeme, Adams, Robert and O'Sullivan, Terence (1994) *Learning How to Learn: Managing Personal and Team Effectiveness, Book 2*, Management Education Scheme by Open Learning (MESOL), Milton Keynes, Open University.

Sarachild, Kathie (1971) 'Consciousness-Raising and Intuition', in Agel (1971).

Sarbin, Theodore R. (1971) 'Self-Reconstitution Processes: A Preliminary Report', *Psychoanalytic Review*, vol. 57, n. 4, pp. 599–615.

Sarbin, T. R. and Adler, N. 1971 'Self-reconstitution Processes: a Preliminary Report', *Psychoanalytic Review*, vol. 57, part 4, pp. 599–615.

Satyamurti, Carole (1981) *Occupational Survival: The Case of the Local Authority and Social Worker*, Oxford, Basil Blackwell.

Schon, Donald A. (1991) *The Reflective Practitioner: How Professionals Think in Action*, Aldershot, Avebury.

Scraton, P., Sim, J. and Skidmore, P. (1991) *Prisons under Protest*, Milton Keynes, Open University Press.

Seligman, M.E.P. (1975) *Helplessness. On Depression, Development and Death*, San Francisco, Freeman.

Shor, I. (1992) *Empowering Education: Critical Teaching for Social Change*, London, University of Chicago Press.

Sidel, Victor W. and Sidel, Ruth (1976) 'Beyond Coping', *Social Policy*, September-October, pp. 67–9.

Silverman, Phyllis R. (1980) *Mutual Help Groups: Organisation and Development*, Beverly Hills, Sage.

Sinclair, Elma (1988), 'The Formal Evidence', in National Institute for Social Work, *Residential Care: A Positive Choice*, London, HMSO.

Sleeter, C. (1991) *Empowerment Through Multi-Cultural Education*, State University of New York, Albany.

Smale, Gerald and Tuson, Graham, with Biehal, Nina and Marsh, Peter (1993) *Empowerment, Assessment, Care Management and the Skilled Worker*, London, HMSO.

Smiles, Aileen (1956) *Samuel Smiles and his Surroundings*, London, Robert Hale.

Smiles, Samuel (1875) *Thrift*, London, Harper & Bros.

Smiles, Samuel (1890) *Self-Help: With Illustrations of Conducts and Perseverance*, London, John Murray.

Smith, Brenda (1989) 'The Case for Women's Studies in Social Work Education', in Helen Marchant and Betsy Wearing (eds), *Gender Reclaimed: Women and Social Work*, Sydney, Hale & Iremonger, pp. 201–11.

Social Work, National Institute for (1982) *Social Workers, Their Role and Tasks (The Barclay Report)*, London, Bedford Square.

Solomon, Barbara Bryant (1976) *Black Empowerment: Social Work in Oppressed Communities* New York, Columbia University Press.

SSI (1991) *Women in Social Services: A Neglected Resource*, London, HMSO.

Stanley, L. and Wise, S. (1983) *Breaking Out: Feminist Consciousness and Feminist Research*, London, Routledge & Kegan Paul.

Stanton, Alan (1990) 'Empowerment of Staff: A Prerequisite for the Empowerment of Users?', in Pam Carter, Tony Jeffs and Mark Smith (eds), *Social Work and Social Welfare Yearbook 2 1990*, Buckingham, Open University Press, pp. 122–33.

Stevenson, O. and Parsloe, P. (1993), *Community Care and Empowerment*, Joseph Rowntree Foundation.

Stewart, A. (1994) *Empowering People*, London, Pitman.

Stokes, Bruce (1981) *Helping Ourselves: Local Solutions to Global Problems*, London, Norton.

Swift, C. and Levin, G. (1987) 'Empowerment: An Emerging Mental Health Technology', *Journal of Primary Prevention*, 8 (1 and 2) (Fall/Winter).

Tax, Sol (1976) 'Self-Help Groups: Thoughts on Public Policy', *Journal of Applied Behavioural Science*, 12, Part 3, pp. 448–54.

Taylor, David (1989) 'Citizenship and Social Power', *Critical Social Policy*, issue 26, vol. 9, no. 2 (Autumn) pp. 19–31.

Thomas, M. and Pierson, J. (1995) *Dictionary of Social Work*, London, Collins Educational.

Thompson, Neil (1993) *Anti-Discriminatory Practice*, London, BASW/Macmillan.

Thorpe, Mary (1993) *Evaluating Open and Distance Learning*, 2nd edn, Harlow, Longman.

Toren, Nina (1972) *Social Work: The Case of a Semi- Profession*, Beverley Hills, Sage.

Towell, David (ed.) (1988) *An Ordinary Life in Practice*, London, King Edward's Hospital Fund.

Townsend, Peter (1979) *Poverty in the United Kingdom*, London, Allen & Unwin.

Tracy, George S. and Gussow Zachery (1976) 'Self-Help Groups: A Grassroots Response to a Need for Services', *Journal of Applied Behavioural Science*, 12, Part 3, pp. 381–96.

Trevillion, S. (1992) *Caring in the Community: A Networking Approach to Community Partnership*, Harlow, Longman.

Turner, Stephen (1994) *The Social Theory of Practices: Tradition, Tacit Knowledge and Presuppositions*, Oxford, Polity Press.

Twelvetrees, Alan (1991) *Community Work*, 2nd edn, London, BASW/Macmillan.

Tyler, Ralph W. (1976) 'Social Policy and Self-Help Groups', *Journal of Behavioural Science*, 23, Part 3, pp. 444–8.

Unell, Judith (1987) *Help for Self-Help: A Study of a Local Support Service*, London, Bedford Square/NCVO.

Ungerson, Clare (1987) *Policy is Personal: Sex, Gender and Informal Care*, London, Tavistock.

User-Centred Services Group, The (1993) *Building Bridges Between People Who Use and People Who Provide Services*, London, NISW.

Vattano, Anthony J. (1972) 'Power to the People: Self-Help Groups', *Social Work*, vol. 17, no. 4 (July) pp. 7–15.

Videka, Lynn M. (1979) 'Psychosocial Adaptation in a Medical Self-Help Group', in Lieberman *et al.* (1979) pp. 362–86.

Walker, H. and Beaumont, B. (1981) *Probation Work: Critical Theory and Socialist Practice*, Oxford, Blackwell.

Wallerstein, N. (1992) 'Powerlessness, Empowerment and Health: Implications for Health Promotion Programs', *American Journal of Health Promotion*, vol. 6, no. 3, pp. 197–205.

Ward, D. (1986) 'Radford Adds New Benefit to a Training Partnership', *Social Work Today*, 1 September, pp. 8–9.

Ward, D. and Mullender, A. (1988) 'The Centrality of Values in Social Work Education', *Issues in Social Work Education*, vol. 8, no. 1, pp. 46–54.

Ward, D. Mullender, A. (1991) 'Empowerment and Oppression: An Indissoluble Pairing for Contemporary Social Work', *Critical Social Policy*, issue 32, vol. 11, no. 2 (Autumn) pp. 21–30.

Webb, Penny (1982) 'Back to Self-Help?', *Royal Society of Health Journal*, 102, Part 3 (June) pp. 124–9.

Wechsler, Henry (1960) 'The Self-Help Organisation in the Mental Health Field: Recovery Inc. A Case Study', *Journal of Nervous and Mental Diseases*, 130, pp. 297–314.

Who Cares? a magazine produced by the Who Cares Trust, 235–245 Goswell Road, London EC1V 7JD, for young people in the care system.

Willen, Mildred L. (1984) 'Parents Anonymous: The Professional's Role as Sponsor', in Gartner and Riessman (1984), pp. 109–19.

Wilson, Judy (1986) *Self-Help Groups: Getting Started – Keeping Going*, Harlow, Longman.

Wilson, Judy (1988) *Caring Together: Guidelines for Carers' Self-Help and Support Groups*, London, King's Fund.

Wilson, Melba (1989) 'Overcoming the Legacy of Child Sexual Abuse', *Social Work Today*, vol. 20, no. 30, pp. 12–13.

Wolfendale, Sheila (1992) *Empowering Parents and Teachers: Working for Children*, London, Cassell.

Wolfenden, Lord (1978) *The Future of Voluntary Organisations: Report of the Wolfenden Committee*, London, Croom Helm.

Wolfensberger, W. (1972) *The Principle of Normalisation in Human Services*, Toronto, National Institute on Mental Retardation.

Wright, N. (1989) *Assessing Radical Education*, Milton Keynes, Open University Press.

Young, Martin and Rigge, Marianne (undated) *Mutual Aid in a Selfish Society: A Plea for Strengthening the Co-operative Movement*, Paper No. 2, London, Mutual Aid Press.

Zimmerman, M. and Rappaport, J. (1988) 'Citizen Participation, Perceived Control and Psychological Empowerment', *American Journal of Community Psychology*, vol. 16, no. 5, pp. 725–50.

Zweig, Marilyn (1971) 'Is Women's Liberation a Therapy Group?', in Agel (1971).

Index